My Brooklyn...
Your Brooklyn

My Brooklyn...
Your Brooklyn

KEVIN J. LEDDY

To order additional copies of this book, contact:
Xlibris
1-888-795-4274
www.Xlibris.com
Orders@Xlibris.com
760973

Contents

I DEDICATE THIS BOOK TO

My Mom and Dad Gene and Peggy

My Brothers and Sisters Michael,Eileen, Maryann and Brian

My Bride Robin

My Children Nicholas, Garrett and Jacqueline

My Nieces and Nephews Michael, Nicole, Genna, Angelica, Marina,Brooke,Brigid,Connor,Sean Arianna and Harley

My Cousins The Gardners, The Wards, The Kehoes, The McMahons and The Nelsons

All The Families on East 55TH Street

Mary Queen of Heaven Class of 1974 and All MQH Alumni

The "L" Park Crew

The Roller Palace Crew

The Ave "N" Crew

And... especially....

Everett Scott

Preface

How many times in your life have you heard this phrase? "When I was growing up things were a lot different than how kids got it today." I know I have heard it and have even said it more times that I care to admit. I have engaged in similar conversations with people of my own age and older comparing the times of yesteryear versus today and it would always produce the inevitable line... Where I grew up...

Well where I grew up was a little place called Brooklyn. Yes Brooklyn, the 4th largest city in America, the bastion of poor and middle class hard working people, the melting pot of all ethnicity, the home of the most diverse culinary offerings, and where the Brooklyn Dodgers played. The descriptions of Brooklyn are numerous and it all depends on who you ask to see what they deem most important to label it.

If you ask me, my answer will be... it was the greatest place on this planet to grow up in... and of course I will always respond with saying... "it's home."

If you grew up in Brooklyn, you have many memories of the events and just everyday life as you lived it day after day. While we were living those Brooklyn days I somehow get the feeling that we, in some distorted way, did not realize the complete wonder of those times. As we lived them it is as if we almost expected that this was the way life was and was going to be for the rest of our lives. Unfortunately times have changed just as our own lives changed, and I say that with no regrets.

I looked back to in my own mind those times and questioned why they were so different from today and really did not come up with a definitive answer. The one constant word that was present and true in every memory I possessed was "Neighborhood." Yes The Neighborhood that to me defines the difference from the times in question. It was where your life took place and it was where all the characters played their roles in your growing up. It was where the milestones of our lives took place. It was where your life lessons were taught and learned in and out of school. It was where your values that you still cherish even to this day were instilled in you. It is where you allowed people, friends family and even strangers into your hearts to play their part in your youthful journey.

Let me just say that if you took two people who grew up in different neighborhoods in Brooklyn and sat them down in a room together they could talk for hours on end and basically share the same stories as if they grew up right next door to each other

You see that is why I am writing this book. The stories that I will share with you as you turn each page do not belong to me exclusively. They are YOUR stories just as much as they are mine. All you really have to do is change the names and faces and use your own neighborhood as their back drop and believe me they are yours. I have included after each story an empty page for you to put your story on it so it will become "Your Brooklyn "and a journal to pass on to those who you wish to remember your story

My recollections of my life in Brooklyn are one of the treasures I call my own .When I verbally shared them with other people not just Brooklynites I got the chance to hear them unanimously agree ...".It is a shame those times are long gone and forgotten" I thought after hearing that. I refused to let those times be forgotten and lost on the next generation. It was then that decided to write these stories down and it was Facebook that I chose as my venue to voice them. After posting my first seven stories people who read them responded by saying "I can't wait to share this with my children. You just described my life growing up on my block." Many of you readers said that I should write a book because of how well it related and verbally illustrated their life and times growing up in Brooklyn and they wished to have a record of them.

Now please let me tell you I don't consider myself an author by any stretch of the imagination. I am just a Brooklyn kid with a decent memory. I will tell you that I didn't even have this book edited as you will find out by all my typos and grammar errors and so forth, but I felt that I wanted to write it as I tawked it.

I also wanted to include all the people who were a part of my life growing up in Brooklyn and those who encouraged me to write this book. Therefore you will find a long list of names on the final pages and your name will be on them. It is my way of saying thanks.

-Kevin J. Leddy... A Brooklyn Kid............Always.

Dijeet Suppa Yet?

I need youse guys to gimme a hand wit dis. You see I have traveled to many places in my life and no matter where I go, it seems the minute I open my mouth to say one word people automatically know that I am from Brooklyn. I believe that in some ways we as Brooklynites have own special language and what people call our "accents", well I never thought I had one while growing up in Brooklyn, I guess to other people I do .I have over the years while living here on "Lawng Giland" thought to have lost my "accent". I don't think I did it with any intention but I think it is because I don't spend as much time with fellow Brooklynites.

"The thing is dis", I "ain't got no problem" with what people think about the way I "tawk" and if they got "beef" with it, well than they could "go scracth" for all I care.

I never thought there was anything "fugazy" about the way we Brooklynites "tawked". So when people from other places would imply that I spoke funny, I would just shake my head and say"git outta here"

I kinda like the fact that we are can be identified by our way of speech because it not only lets us identify each other it also gives a sense of camaraderie, it also gives us all a sense of pride and uniqueness. I have known people who intentionally attempt to hide and conceal their so called "accent" because to some people it is a sign of lower intelligence and class (Dem people ain't got the stones to say it to our faces though). Some people embrace it like I do and speak with my "accent" as if it were a badge of honor. Unfortunately because of the migration from Brooklyn to places like "Lawng Giland" and New Joisey" our native "accents" and unique sayings are in jeopardy of being just another memory. I hope and pray that never happens

I hope that all the wonderful sayings and our "strange" pronunciations we have in Brooklyn will always be remembered even if they are these days rarely spoken. There are some things that if said to anyone else, anywhere on this planet, they would look at you as if you just grew anther head.

For instance

Didja have a "cuppa cawfee" in the morning witcha "bealley"? Do ya put a "courtta earl" in ya car every "wounceinawhile"? When yous were a kid didja Mutta carry a "poccabook"?

Didja know anybody who lived on ThoidyThoid St.? Jeet Suppa yet?

I could go on and on with so many other examples of our beloved Brooklyn language and the things that stick in my mind, I will leave it up to youse guys to remember your own. What I really enjoy most when I think of these old sayings is the people who said them

While our language may not be the most elegant, nor the sweetest sounding Itis ours and I embrace it I hope it will stand the test of time and be spoken forever.

So the next time you find yourself away from the beautiful confines of our beloved Brooklyn and some guy in a straw hat and a pair of overalls asks you "You sure do speak funny, where are you from?"....Just look him right in the eye and say....Fuggitaboutit.

Tell me some of the sayings you relate to Brooklyn.

Your Brooklyn

Where Is This Place We Are Eating?

I am 6 years old .It is a Friday night in our Brooklyn home which meant it was a pay day for my Dad. We sit on the couch in the living room waiting for him to arrive home which is normally around 6:30 or 7 O'clock. I join Michael on the floor in front of our console television set made by Sylvania as we hold our chins in our hands and our legs go up and down as if we were riding an imaginary bicycle as we watch Speed Racer as he attempts to reveal the secret identity of the mysterious Racer X on Channel 9 WOR .We are extra excited tonight because some reason Mom is not cooking dinner and it would appear that there are other plans that we kids have not learned of yet. My sister Eileen gets up to look out the picture window because she said she heard a car door and we all wait for her to report as to whether or not it is Dad or not....she turns with an ear to ear smile and squeals...." He is home....It's Dad !!! Michael and me jump to our feet and rush to the front door .Michael opens the inside door and we all jockey for position at the "Storm Door" window to be the first to wave to him as he gets to the stoop. He climbs the stoop opens the door as he does we all jump into his arms and beg him to tell us why he called and told Mom not to cook? Michael swears we are getting Pizza...Eileen says it's gonna be Chinese food... as we bombard him with our guesses. He calmly says "All of you must go upstairs put your Sunday clothes on and make sure we are all washed and clean". And then he would take us in the car to answer all our questions. We all dressed as quick as humanly possible as Mom dressed Maryann .We all leave our house through the front door and Michael is the last out and Morn says" Make sure the inside door is locked "Michael does as he is told and with the house secure we all pile into the Plymouth station wagon, Morn is carrying Maryann in her arms so Dad holds the car open for her as she get in and keeps Maryann on her lap (no car seat). Dad close the door after telling Morn to "Watch your feet" and then comes around and assumes his position in the driver's seat and we are off. We drive down to Ave N and Dad parks the car in the Boback parking lot. We all get out and cross the Ave and head towards this building with a green and red neon sign it its window

Michael runs ahead to open the door for everyone, because that is what a gentleman does according to Dad I am holding my Morns hand as she follows Dad and the rest of the family into this strange building. Dad turns to me and my older brother and sister and says" Now I need you guys to behave yourselves". We all knew what that meant by the look in his eye when he said it. A man greets us at the door and shows us to a table and we all sit down. As I look around the room I can see people sitting at other tables eating food. But I don't know any of them and am wondering why they are here. I am sitting at Kings Restaurant on Ave N in Brooklyn. This is very strange to me when Morn asks me what I want to eat. I say "I will eat anything you are cooking Mom". Laughter followed.

I write this just to show that when I grew up in Brooklyn going out to eat was such a special event and not the weekly norm in life today. Somewhere along the way we lost the Family

Dinner at Home and what it meant to us and what it has cost us as Families. Nowadays eating with all your family around the table at home is as foreign as I felt that day at Kings. Do you miss the dinners that I speak of or do you enjoy the convenience of restaurants and fast food chains?

Your Brooklyn

Manners Were Taught Early In Brooklyn

Growing up in Brooklyn some of my earliest memories were that of Kiddie Birthday parties. On my block there were at least I would say 15 boys and girls my age. I am talking now about the age of 5-7.

I recall my Mom taking me to the "5 and Dime" (Aveys) on Ave N and Ralph Ave to shop for a gift for whichever friends birthday was to be celebrated. She would let me look up and down the aisle of toys to see what I thought that friend would want. Of course I always picked out something that I wanted, knowing that he would let me play with it in our respective backyards when the Birthday Party was over. It's funny how we start thinking this way even at 6 years old.

Back home my Mom wraps the gift with such tender loving care and painstaking skill to get the ribbon to curl just right. Meanwhile I am thinking how silly she is because I know Joe Duval (the Birthday boy Du Jour) is going to rip that paper and ribbons to shreds in8 seconds flat!

Gift under arm combed hair and clean outfit I set out on the long journey of walking 4 doors down to Joes. I tum down his alleyway and see on the back fence an accordion style HAPPY BIRTHDAY sign in blue letters hanging on the gate it tells me I am in the right place. I open the back gate and walk into the backyard and this is what greets my eyes. There balloons and twisted Crepe Paper and there are two picnic tables covered with paper ...(Happy Birthday printed) tables cloths with paper cups and napkins and a mysterious folded at the top paper "Goodie" bag each proclaiming the same message. There are two huge "Tupperware bowls, one filled with Potato Chips (Charles Chips out of the big tin) and the other with Pretzels. In the center of the table is the Birthday Cake displayed in all it's sugary icing glory There is a portable record player on the back stoop playing party songs but later to be used when we play the overly competitive game of "Musical Chairs. We all are having a ball playing, then Joe opens his gifts and just as I thought,Joe destroyed my Moms wrapped masterpiece in under 8 seconds .Simon Says and all the traditional games have been played except one.....It was always the highlight of every kiddie party .....yes there would be a prize for the talented kid who could be blessed with the remarkable skill of having been blind folded ...spun around 5 times and with a thumbtack or piece of scotch tape in his or her hand and have the wherewithal to pin a tail on the butt of a paper donkey!!!!!

We sing song the proverbial Happy Birthday as Mrs. Duval lit the candles on the cake...we shout in synchronized voices...How old are you now?"

We all have our cake and the finale is near we all line up at the back gate and as we exit and thank Joe for having us at his party and of course you Thank Mrs. Duval... because the last thing your Mom said to you before you left the house to go to the party was "Make sure you thank Joe's mother when you leave". I as expected forgot and had to run back and Thank Mrs. Duval and ask her to tell my Mom that I didn't forget. We all receive that Mysterious Goodie bag which brings this wonderful party to it's completion and race home to open it up and reveal the treasures that are within. What a day!!! Now I start thing who is next to have a birthday, I know that I just I can't wait for mine.

Oh by the way I went to a little 5 year olds birthday party yesterday...I watched 20 kids jump in a Bounce Castle and play video games.

Do you remember those old parties as I did?

Your Brooklyn

A Day in Kindergarten At PS 203 Brooklyn

It's 8:30 A.M. on a sunny Brooklyn morning and it seems very strange to me at 5 years old to have to dress up on a Monday? You see my Mom tells me I am going to meet new friends and I am going to play and learn all kinds of new games and others things. She explains to me that I will be staying there for the whole morning but I would be coming home for lunch. So I begin what will turn out to be my everyday ritual that will be a part of my life for at least the next 13years......getting ready for SCHOOL... because today I am going to Kindergarten!!!!

My shorts are pressed as is my short sleeve button down shirt and shoes are shined to a high gloss finish... and on they go, which usually is reserved for Church on Sunday yet that will be my attire as I enter this brand new world. Into my hair goes that "greasy kid stuff" Mom combs it with tender loving care to make sure I look my best as will every other Mom of the kids I am soon to meet.

Mom announces we are ready and our journey to Kindergarten begins, we walk the short 4 blocks from 55th St to 5tst St stopping at each corner so Mom could hold my hand as we crossed........ I take it upon myself to look both ways in a "I am protecting Mom kinda way" There she stands....its 3 stories seem huge as my eyes take in the building and it's entirety......P.S. 203!!!!!We enter the schoolyard and I see more kids than I ever saw in one place before in my life...there were MILLIONS!!!...well it seemed that way to this 5 year old. We lined up in front of a woman who held up a sign that read ..." Kindergarten A.M. #111• Her name was Mrs. Siegel and the minute I stood in front of her and waved bye to Mom there was no doubt I was not a baby anymore I was a 'Schoolkid" like all the other kids on my block.

Mrs. Siegel walked us to our classroom and assigned us a place to sit. There were five tables in the classroom each was adorned with a center piece that was either Red,Blue,Yellow, Green or Purple. I was to be a member of the "Yellow" table. To this very day yellow is my favorite color and I often wonder if there was a connection. Anyway I look around this strange place called the "Classroom" and I see wooden blocks, I see jars of paints and paintbrushes, I see "construction paper" in every color but most of all I see the biggest box of "Crayola" crayons I ever saw in all my short life. There is one or two kids that are just not ready for this place and are crying and upset. Mrs. Siegel comforts them as if they were her own children....I know right then I am going to like her, she's nice.

She addresses our class and lets us know we are free to play with whatever we please but we are to share and be nice to one another. She then makes us all stand up at our table place our right hand over our hearts and face the American flag hanging in the middle of the chalkboard directly over it and we pledged our allegiance to that flag in our sing song kinda way and that was to be performed everyday ...and it was for every day of my scholastic career until college. I choose to color which I love to do. So there I was sitting with 4 other kids with our heads and faces as close to the paper as humanly possible coloring a picture of our homes as suggested by Mrs. Siegel. She stops by the yellow table and shows us all a little trick.... She makes a half circle in the right hand corner of the paper I am drawing on and colors it in yellow and drew for 6 straight little lines coming away from it and there was..."The Sun". I thought that was the coolest thing I ever saw. The only thing I can actually say that I really did not like in Kindergarten was the taste of the white "Elmer's Glue Paste" when I licked the orange applicator which was also the lid!!! Tell the truth ...You tasted it too...didn't you? Be honest!!!

Your Brooklyn

Yes In My Brooklyn We Talked To Each Other and We Listened

We live in a world of amazing technology today. It would seem that we can see, hear or know about anything happening in this world within 10 minutes of it taking place. Our cell phones enable us instant knowledge of any of our friends and families activities and inquiries. The internet provides us with the news of world events in real time. Our televisions in this day and age with all its glorious 999 channels ensures us that you can't miss any current events even if you tried to avoid them. I just wonder how in God's name did we ever do without them? Well this is how I recall doing without them

It is 1971 March 8th to be exact Everett Scott Michael Mike Nelson Glen Nelson Michael Brennan, Joe Joseph Duval, Michael Mike Miello and Kenny Kenneth Spinelli and all the other guys on my block are gathered in my basement as my brother Michael grabs our kitchen and dining room chairs and in Ford assembly line fashion they are handed down the stairs and set up against the walls of our basement. My Mom is busy filling bowls lined with napkins with Charles Chips and Bachmann's Pretzels. Paper cups provided by a company called Dixie were there to hold the White Rock sodas in assorted flavors Cola, Lemon-Lime, Orange, Root Beer or Imitation Grape that came in a can and you needed a metal can opener(Church Key). We all sat around eating those snacks and drinking our sodas and arguing over what we thought would be the results of what we all gathered here for.

Then it was time, Michael took one of Moms Snack Tables (T.V. Dinner Tables) and placed it in the middle of all of us as we sat along the basement walls. An extension cord was run over to the socket under my Dads workbench and plugged into the socket at the other end of that extension cord was a square fake snakeskin covered box with a metal antenna rising up from its base, it had a clear plastic front with numbers and letters and a dial that moved a thin red line behind the plastic to the desired numbers representing the station you wished to listen to. Behind the box a little snap was opened and revealed a compartment which housed a plug and cord as well as a compartment for batteries (8 D 'S). Michael then plugged the two cords together and set the dial to 770 WABC and then the distinctive voice of Howard Cosell could be heard from this box in the center of my basement floor .This was the night of The Fight Of The Century. Smokin Joe Frazier was fighting Mohammed Ali for the Heavy Weight Championship of the World. It was not to be broadcast on television and was only shown in pay per view at your local Movie Theater for $20!!! Who had $20 to spend to see a fight? I know none of the guys on my block did and so here we were sitting in my basement just staring at a box on a table and listening intensely to the description Mr. Cosell painted in our minds. We all jumped up in between rounds and shadow boxed with each other and claimed how we could beat both of those fighters for the money they were making (Yea sure). So there we sat for 14 rounds and then Joe Frazier reached down all the way to Georgia and grabbed himself a hook, he pulled it up through the Carolinas and through Virginia and Maryland it swept through New Jersey and came into New York right into the most famous arena in the world (Madison Square Garden) and landed it on the jaw of one Mohammed Ali and buckled his knees sending him to the canvas. The 15th round was anticlimactic, then Don Dunphy took the descended microphone in his hand and announced that by way of unanimous decision......The winner and STILL Champion... Joe Frazier!!!

That night 12 young men sat around in a basement staring at a box and listened to a fight and had the best time of their lives, without a cell phone, without a TV, and without video games. This wonderful device could do all the things all the aforementioned things could do with all their technological advances. It could be found on every red and white checkered tablecloth covered Bar-BQue. It could be noticed on the front stoop every evening as the neighbors gathered to talk to each other. It was a constant in the kitchen as the family meals were being prepared. It was ever present on the beaches from Manhattan Beach to Riess Park and The Rockaways .We found our news from John Montone(1010) We heard about The Yanks and the Mets from Phil Rizzuto(WPIX) and Ralph Kiner (WOR) and the music that soothe our souls could be played by The WMCA Good Guys. That's right you guessed it...The Radio...Yes the Radio with its two music stations WMCA AND WABC...Yes the Radio with its two sports stations WOR and WPIX and yes the radio with its two new stations WINS AND WCBS. The radio was enough for us even with its limitations because we also did something else back then that is quite strange by today's standards...We Talked to each other!!!!I must however admit that the technology of today has made us much more informed than any generation before and I am not sure that is such a good thing. My world was barely touched by any events outside of Brooklyn and I think I was alright with that growing up ...but was that a good thing either?

Your Brooklyn

"Here's A Little Something for You"

"Here's a little something for you." Growing up in Brooklyn these six words were said often and instituted a ritual that is rarely performed today.

You see when I was growing up in Brooklyn people worked at whatever job they had and were proud to be earning a living no matter what your trade was. What really impressed me was that we all appreciated what others did, and what we could try to let them know it.

Whether it be your Family Doctor who would come to visit a sick family member at your home to the men who picked up and emptied your metal garbage cans.

The very first time I experienced this ritual was when I was about 6 years old and I was driving in our Plymouth station wagon with my Dad and we stopped at the gas station to fill up with gas. The man in his blue overalls with a big red star on his chest (TEXACO) greeted my Dad with a smile and a "How you doin Pal, what will it be?" .My Dad replied "five bucks regular (which would fill the tank) and could you check under the hood?" The man in the overalls went to work, he started the pump after inserting the nozzle into the gas tank. He then proceeds to pop open the hood and check the earl (oil), his head sticks out from the side of the open front hood and announces to my Dad that he is a quart low and asks if he should put one in. Dad gives the OK and two minutes later the hood is closed and he is on to his next task. Window washing fluid is sponged onto the windshield and then he takes a rag and wipes them dry and spotless. The man the approaches my Dad in the driver's window and says "That'll be five dollars."

My Dad hands him a five dollar bill and then hands the man two quarters and says "Here a little something for you". As we drove away I asks my Dad why he gave that man the two quarters. He explained to me that when people do things for you in life no matter whether it is their job to do so or not, always let them know that they are appreciated.

I began to notice that this practice was a part of our everyday Brooklyn lives. When my Mom would make the pay envelope for the Milkman (Put into the metal milk box and left OUTSIDE OVERNIGHT! !!) she would ask my Dad for a "little something extra for the Milkman .When the person who bagged our groceries at the A&P Mom would slip them a nickel and say "Here's a little something for you". The paper delivery boy every Friday night would "get a little something for himself. The Charles Chip delivery guy always got "A little something for him" as did the knife sharpening man in his green truck even the U.P.S. man was always given "a little something for himself. It did not necessarily always have to be a monetary reward. My Mom would always have a glass of cold water for our Mailman on hot summer days, I even remember Mom making lunch for the guys who installed our water heater. I thought the coolest by far was when Dad took me and my brother Michael to Shea Stadium to watch the Mets and the Usher would greet us. Dad would fold a buck in his hand and then shake the Ushers hand like no one needed to know kinda way and say "Thanks Pal and here's a little something for you"(I refer to that as "Old Brooklyn Style"), as he led us to our seats.

I fear today we have left this ritual behind us for no other reason than the fact we are no longer as connected to those who perform services for us in daily lives .So here is my question....Who do you say "Here's a little something for you" these days and do you recall some of the memories that I did?

Your Brooklyn

BROOKLYN MADE YOU THINK OUTSIDE THE BOX

There is starting to get a little chill in the air on an October day in Brooklyn. I am 10 years old and am heading home from school with my schoolbag in hand that resembles a briefcase with a double hard plastic handles and a flap over leather strap with its metal lock attachment. Inside that schoolbag were textbooks and marble notebooks for each subject from Mathematics to Phonics and Science. My schoolbag was pretty heavy to say the least, so heavy that every block or so on that journey home I had to stop to switch hands holding it. I am almost home as I turn the corner and walk down "myblock", the last leg of my journey. I spot something that immediately brings a smile to my face. There, parked right in front of the Scotts house, is a Sears Roebuck appliance truck!!! Now to kids today this would mean absolutely nothing but to a kid from Brooklyn in my day it meant a world of adventure was about to begin.

The refrigerator that was to be the Scotts brand new home addition is now going into their front door(screen door had to be removed to fit it through the door). I pick up my schoolbag with both arms and race down my block to my house to drop off my books, change out of my school uniform into my play clothes and try to be the first kid to make it to the front of the Scotts house. With my school uniform thrown about my bedroom and school shoes landing somewhere separately in my wake I bound down the stairs and make a Beeline for the front door only to stop for a quick kiss for my Mom. "Would you like a quick snack? "Mom asks "No thanks Mom the Scotts got a new refrigerator ". She knows what that means and watches me burst out the front door and all I can hear Mom saying is something about not letting the screen door slam ....as it slams shut... ooops sorry Mom.

It looked like the opening bell at a thoroughbred race at Aqueduct Racetrack as every kid on my block was sprinting out their front door like they were galloping out the gate at the track just like me all at about the same time. We all converge on the Scotts house (the finish line so to speak) and there it is the object that will be our magical obsession for this day

...The Refrigerator Box!!!

You see to us this was no ordinary box no sir .This box was going to be a Fort to be defended from our imaginary attackers. This box was going to be our study ship sailing on our sea of black tar. This box was going to be our shelter from the made up storms. This box was going to be a sled that magically glides on asphalt. The box was going to be a hiding place. This box was going to be anything we wanted it to be .The possibilities were endless. This box was about to be tested by all the kids on my block and it did not disappoint. Within two hours of playing with "The Refrigerator Box" it would finally start to give into our relentless abuse. It would start to rip, and its shape was no longer that study tall rectangular place of adventure it was now becoming just some old cardboard to be discarded in the trash. But for two and a half hours it kept twenty kids on my block under its spell and inspired our imaginations to its furthest reaches.

I am a grown man now with three grown kids of my own. I often wish that if a Genie were to emerge from a lamp that I just happened to rub, I would wish to have my kids come back in time with me, so I could share with them the magic of playing in the street with The Refrigerator Box.

I have often since seen PC Richards and still Searstrucks delivering appliances and I never fail to smile to myself and think about playing in one just one more time. You see when we were kids we thought "outside the box" but we also thought inside the box as well.

Did you share this memory as I do?

Your Brooklyn

Easter Sundays in Brooklyn

Growing up in my beloved Brooklyn I never knew the difference of all the Religions that shared the geographically small corner of the world that I inhabited.

I am 10 years old so it is 1970 in the world's largest ethnic melting pot we called home. I can't speak for other young men of other faiths so I can only relate to you what my views were and just how it affected my experience as I was coming of age in the greatest little city on this planet.

My Dad was a New York City Fireman so that meant he got his paycheck every other week as was the law of New York State and all its employees, whether you be a Police Officer or Sanitation worker and or any other person who worked for the State.

Now that being said I relate to you the chaos that that caused in my home when March gave way to April and Easter Season was thrust upon us as a family was unbearable.

To most Irish, Italian, Polish, English and every other nationality that fell under the umbrella of Christianity the Easter season was a major financial burden that was accepted as just "our way of life" and being paid every other week only added to the interruption of our lives

You see in my beloved Brooklyn, and I am willing to bet on every corner of this planet where Christians gathered Easter Sunday for some reason became a day of pageantry and like every good Christian family we adhered to its tradition.

This particular year Dad got paid on Good Friday and the stores were all closed by the time my Mom was able to hold in her hand the cashed check from the New York City Fire Dept. which meant we had to shop for our Easter Outfits on Saturday, the very day before Easter Sunday..

Now I don't know if you realize exactly what that meant to a woman who had five children that needed to be dressed for Easter Sunday but I will let you know it was far from easy.

Saturday morning following Good Friday was the very first day of our Easter Vacation from school and we, as grade school children, welcomed the break and looked forward to the fun things that were to follow on "Our Block". Only for me and my brothers and sisters it was to be a day spent shopping for our Easters outfits due to the pay schedule of New York State. There was to be no fun until our outfits were selected and hanging in our closets or at the foot of our bunkbeds in mine and my brothers Michael and Brian Leddy case.

We the children of this mother with the determination of making sure her children were not to be viewed as vagabonds on Easter Sunday ceremoniously marched down East 55th Street to the bus stop on Ave N and stood there waiting for the ever present and reliable Flatbush Ave B-41 Bus to deliver us to downtown Brooklyn to A&S or Gimbels or Mays(whichever had the best sales) on Fulton Street .My Mom knew exactly where to shop for each one of her kids and knew which store harbored the best discounts, she was great at that. Now please keep in mind it was Friday that my Dad got paid and living from Paycheck to Paycheck we were shopping THE Saturday before Easter therefore sizes were not abundant and the selections were minimal and not to mention, whatever purchases were made ...there was no time for alterations!!!

Morn was like a General as she commanded the troops (me and my brothers and sisters) from one Department store to the next department store. Knowing to herself that if she did not maximize her savings on each one of us kids with what limited funds she had (and my baby sister Maryann Leddy was a constant effort because this year she was a ....6X... the hardest size on the planet to find yet Morn was up to the task and knew Korvettes was the place to find it), there was a strong chance we would not have enough for the bus ride home after the subway and we all be walking home from the Junction on Nostrand Ave and Flatbush Ave. Easter Sunday arrived the very next Morning and we all stood in the living room wearing our brand new Easter outfits ...my brothers and I in our bell bottomed slacks with patterned sport coats and my sisters in their dresses bonnets and pocketbooks with white Patent Leather shoes and awaited Moms inspection, We performed this ritual every Sunday, but this day was no ordinary Sunday, and we were all well aware of its magnitude.

You see back in the days that I speak of there was not a lot for Moms to showcase what they accomplished on a daily basis. There were no awards for the cleanest home, or the whitest sheets, or the cleanest sidewalk or the shiniest dining room table, or the clearest windows, or the best crease in her children's ironed pair of pants or the taste of the magnificent meals she prepared 365 days a year. However on this day every other Mom looked over every child including her own and others and judged them just to see if she herself was up to par. This I believe at the time was the closest thing to "'The Mom Olympics" to be honest. I might be just a tad prejudiced but I always thought myself and my brothers and sisters to be the best dressed and best groomed of all my friends and classmates ....and for that Mommy ....Thank You.

Later on in life, somewhere around the time I was 14 years old after Easter Sunday took on a whole different meaning to me. After dinner I was allowed to go out to meet up with my friends and I realized I no longer hated the shopping for Easter outfits because I now appreciated new clothes and looked forward to sporting a new outfit and hoped it would impress 14 year old girls who normally got to see me in my street clothes or Uniform.

By the time I turned 14 years old Easter Sunday after dinner became an event of different proportions, You see at that age the girls were corning of age and we as adolescent young men or at least we thought we were, looked forward to seeing the girls whom we hung around with wearing a dress or a skirt. So to Christine Destefano Joyce Cataldo,Lori Cook,Lori Merritt, Diana Pimenta Patty Reda Linda Jones Linda Puma Carol Bozza Missy Kuzinski Katie Mullady. Norine Lombardi-, Fran Mangano. Kitty Zacharias, Irene Cuccurullo and Gina Farley and all the beautiful Brooklyn Princesses I did not name ...Thank You for making every young Brooklyn guys dreams come true by just being the beautiful girls that you all were who dressed up on Easter Sunday!!!!!

I would be remiss if I did not mention the culinary traditions that were sure to a major part of every Easter Celebration. In my home it was always a Leg of Lamb as the prevalent main course with mashed potatoes (It's an Irish Thing) and mint jelly and I still carry that tradition in my own family today (although my daughter Jacqueline has a problem with the whole "lamb issue') and hope it will be passed on.

I would also like to state that it was the Easter season that I first experienced that being a Christian did not give me sole possession of God, for that same year in 1970 I spent a day in my pals home. His name was Richard Silovitz and I was lucky and blessed enough to be invited to Passover service at his home. His Grandfather in his best English (he was a Polish Jew) explained to me the meaning of Passover and enlightened me to the fact that there were other ways to honor and pray to God no matter what or who you were.

Yes my friends Brooklyn provided us all with the opportunity to worship and honor our Gods... but in my case and I am sure many others .... she provided an opportunity for all of us who lived in her boundaries to see others and know that as we were sometimes different....we were that much the same

May God Bless all who seek his blessing just as Brooklyn allowed me to do ....Happy Easter to all and a Blessed Passover to all and especially Haim Silovitz for his time and patience with this Goyim.

Your Brooklyn

Never "Nothing To Do" Growing Up In Brooklyn

My Mom would say... "If you think you are going to sit around the house on a beautiful day like this, you have another thought coming to you Mister"...Now go out and play."

It was an order. Not a suggestion.

I didn't want to go outside ...there was nothing to do out there I said under my breath just low enough for Mom not to here.... "Well it's better than doing nothing in here, at least you will be getting some fresh air" was her response. Yep Moms heard everything no matter how low you talk.

So on go my Keds and out the door I go. I jump from the third step of my stoop and land in a marvelous place known as "Outside"

As I walked along the side walk up and down the street, I looked for something to do. And see what other kids are doing.

Glen Nelson and Mike Nelson are hammering a broken skate on a 2x4 and a milk crate The Connor brothers are flipping Baseball cards with Ray Harrington and Ray is a little worried because he is playing with his brother Michaels Yankee collection.

The Baxter boys Timmy Kevin and Jerry are transforming their front stoop into an army fortress as a game of "Army' was about to be played out with plastic rifles and water guns The Mclinden girls were in front of their house with a jump rope tied to their gate as they skipped as the other turn the jump rope sing songing something about some girl named Miss Mary Mack....

Mary Beth Brown was teaching her little sister Coleen the tedious game of Hopscotch as she stood on one foot as she leaned over to pick up a little stick lying inside a numbered box' James Brennan has his baseball glove on one hand and a Spauldeen in the other and is gathering some kids to play Diamond(running bases)

P.J. Joyce just hit a ball two sewers with a broomstick with black electrical tape on its handle but Paul Rasmussen caught with his bare hand reaching over Mrs. Ritter's fence

Linda Brennan-Burke is playing her new 45s in her alleyway with her portable record player as the beautiful voice of Miss Diana Ross is telling everyone who can hear her song the "There Ain't No Mountain High Enough" can be heard.

Eddie Carloni is riding his bike down the middle of the street just a few feet ahead of Chris Smith on his brand new StingRay

Mike Miello is melting a crayon into a bottle cap as Joe Duval chalks out a new Skully Board in the street.

Barbara Tolan is chasing a Butterfly with a homemade net. (Baby carriage netting on a wire Stephanie Barker-Phillips and my sister Eileen are playing "Hit The Penny" Ken Spinelli Chris Brown and Brian McHenry and playing "BoxBall"

Everett Scott and Michael Brennan are in an intense game of "StoopBall" Mike pretending to be Mickey Mantle and Everett ...Tom Seaver.

Linda Scott and Denise Miello- are playing some card game on her stoop... so Linda could "Check out" Mike Brennan .They were my block's "Sweethearts".

Mrs. Timmons is yelling at Keith Tolan as he climbs her fence to get the whiffle ball that landed in her rose garden (a ground rule double).

Doug and Kenny Robinson were on their skates and shooting a roll of electrical tape in between two garbage cans as their sister Mary Beth Robinson would yell a warning to both of them to "watch out for the cars"

Joann Reda and Terry Tolan are chasing each other trying not to be frozen in "Freeze Tag"

I am pretty sure that what I have just written happened on a daily basis on every block in every Brooklyn neighborhood from Marine Park to Sheepshead Bay and from Mill Basin to Bensonhurst or any other neighborhoods you care to mention and recall... I know that if you all just closed your eyes for a moment you could picture every scene I just described and you have only to change the names and it would be a damn close painted picture of a day in your life on your block where you grew up.

Just doing these simple things were what the magic of growing up in Brooklyn was all about. The menu of activities were endless and the there was never a lack of friends to share them with .The humming sounds of kids playing will forever be the warmest memory I will cherish from my magical childhood growing up in Brooklyn.

I feel such joy when I recall "A Day in the Life on My Block" in Brooklyn and at the same time feel such sorrow for the kids today who only have a computer and an I-Pad.

I think I will take playing outside...Thanks Mom for making me go outside!!!

So here is my question did you play any of these games or did you stay inside?

Your Brooklyn

In Brooklyn Being with Your Family Was Always Special

It is a Friday around 4 O'clock in my house on East 55TH Street in in the summer of 1968. My brother Michael asks my Mom if it would be alright if he could eat dinner at the Nelsons which is a usual occurrence because his best friend is Mike Nelson and every Friday night either my brother eats there or Mike eats at our house. Only this time my Mom says" "No not tonight Michael, when your Dad gets home from work in a little while he says he has a surprise for us."

The news of "Dads surprise" spreads though the house like wildfire and my brothers and sisters are excited and mostly curious. So between Michael, my sister Eileen and me, the whole block within 15 minutes knew my Dad was coming home with a surprise Meanwhile my Mom was ever so nonchalantly making sandwiches in the kitchen and placing them into a plaid soft plastic lunch bag and its matching plaid thermos filled with Sunny Dew Orange drink. We were all so fixed on Dad and his surprise to notice the clues Mom was throwing out as she told us to wash up and change into clean clothes.

It's 6:30 and the anticipation is building by the minute. We are sitting on the stoop with our necks strained to be the first one to see Dads car come up the street. Eileen is the one to spot the Midnight Blue Plymouth Custom Suburban Station Wagon with Dad behind the wheel as he pulled up in front of our house. We rush the car like it's Christmas and the car is the Tree with the presents under it. Dad smiles and says "Everyone jump in ". Mom emerges from the front screen door and with the big lunch bag and thermos and "pocca-book" in hand locks the door and down the stoop and into the car where she takes her rightful seat next to Dad and we are ready to as we are already in our seats and waving to our friends on the street as we leave the block.

Dad navigates the station wagon onto the Belt Parkway and we are heading east towards Long Island we drive for seems to be hours because of the mystery and anticipation. We pull off the Belt and onto Sunrise Highway and before we know it we are behind a long line of cars waiting to enter what seems to be a huge parking lot. The sun is just about down now and darkness is falling. We pull up to a wooden toll booth like building my Dad hands the man some money and into the big parking lot we go. We turn to the left after entering and there it is....the biggest screen I ever saw in my life!!!!!!!!It was huge....It was fantastic.....It was incredible ...It was a surprise alright ...It was ...The Drive In!!!

We were jumping in our seats and cheering Dad for his surprise and pretending to be mad at Mom for keeping it secret. The sandwiches and the Sunny Dew was distributed to each of us as Dad put the speaker on the window of the car. I don't think I could ever recall a happier time than that night as we all heard Charlton Heston say "Take your filthy hands off of me you dirty Ape"

The ride home consisted of us recalling our favorite parts of the movie and which friend we were going to tell first about "Dads Surprise"

Do you remember your first Drive-In Movie? Keep it cleans Guys lol

Your Brooklyn

The B-41 Was Always There For Me In Brooklyn ...She Was My Friend

I am seven years old and it's a beautiful Sunday morning in Brooklyn which is just about to give way to a beautiful afternoon in Brooklyn. I am pacing in front of my house on 55th St occasionally running up the stoop to peak through the screen door to see if Mom had finished the breakfast dishes so we could get on our way. Sundays were always a special day around my house ...but that is a story I will tell another day. Today you will read about one of my oldest and dearest friends.

The fifteen minute wait for Mom, which to me at seven seemed like ours is over. She emerges from the front door, "Poccabook" in hand, "Ready? "she says, I almost shout in return "Yep" as the anticipation was building. We head out down the block towards Ave N.

We arrive and I know right where to stand thanks to the yellow painted curb. My Mom says to me what she says every Sunday. "You can lean over the curb to look, but don't you dare step into that street Mister."

So there I stand leaning over that yellow painted curb and squinting so hard it hurt my eyes. My heart begins to beat a little faster, I think I can see her...Yes!!! It's her. As she gets closer by the block I can see her beautiful Green paint and Chrome shinning and reflecting the sun from the glass windows...The B-41!!! Yes the B-41 bus!!! The door is opened by the driver (not automatically) with a long bar attached from his driver's seat, and then my grandma steps of the bus and I jump into hers arms squealing "Hi Grandma" (I know she has a little something for me for meeting her at the Bus Stop). She reaches into her "Poccabook" and hands me a box of ...Crackerjacks" ...Candy coated popcorn peanuts and a prize.......my favorite!!!

The B-41 was a constant companion throughout my life growing up in Brooklyn. She got me and my family to the places we had to go. She was there when the blizzards came and she made sure Dad got to work. She was there when Mom would take me and my two brothers and sisters to get our Easter clothes at Mays downtown because they were the cheapest. She was there to take us every September to get our school uniforms for at Ideals and Money Savers (shoes) she was there every morning to take me to high-school as long as I showed my pass and gave her a nickel. She was also there for me to jump on the back of her when I didn't have the nickel(totally illegal I might add) She was there when I had to go downtown to get my working papers so I could work at the Male Shop. She was there to get me to The Empire Roller Skating Rink so I could skate the night away she was there when I had to go to Motor Vehicles to get my driver's license. She was also there when I had to go pay my first speeding ticket because Dad took away my driving privileges. She was there when as a man and father I took my son on her to go to the Prospect Park Zoo. Yes the B-41was not just a bus ...she was my friend.

What bus was your friend?

Your Brooklyn

Brooklyn Markets on Your Street

KEVIN LEDDY·FRIDAY, APRIL 28, 2017

Growing up in Brooklyn I remember a rather strange fact that by today's standards is almost unheard of. I guess it was partly because men were still considered to be the "bread winners" and woman often the the caregivers and also managed the household. Maybe it was just that we in Brooklyn as a society had not evolved yet and women were still not considered equal to men. Mind you the traditional family hierarchy was very much controlled by the fathers in the homes for better or worse. I don't recall many mothers on my block that drove cars!. Now take a moment to let that set in, I don't know how it was on your block but I can only remember four Moms who drove on mine and we had forty-six families living there. Now think about how Mothers today would be able to survive without being able to drive and perform their errands on a daily basis. I have a theory as to how our Moms made it all work for them without the use of a car back in those glorious days growing up in Brooklyn. It is Sunday night in my house and my brothers and sisters and myself have finished the nightly routine of taking our baths or showers. We walk up to Mom as she sits at the dinning room table writing on a piece of paper. She interrupts her writing for each of us as we put our hands out so she can make sure we cleaned our fingernails and inspected our necks especially behind our ears to make sure we washed properly and were ready for school the next morning. Mom had just finished her writing as I,,the last to pass inspection will be entrusted to put that note in it's rightful place.So I open the front screen door and step out and there she sits. It was a silver metal 14"x14x14"" styrofoam insulated top lidded box that was a constant and sat outside on every stoop on my block. Into that box went the paper that Mom told me to put in it...it read ....Four bottles of Milk...... One pound of Butter One dozen Eggs. In the morning like magic those items would appear in the Milk Box and breakfast was ensured. The Milkman delivered. Monday morning a blue rather large truck would come down the block with "General Diaper Service" written on it with a picture of a cute little baby in a diaper wearing a military Generals hat. There were no Pampers or Huggies then, there were cloth diapers that had to be washed and General provided the pick up and delivery service. Tuesday a green truck with an open back and open side windows would beep his horn as he drove down the block Mothers would appear in front of that truck with their kitchen knives and scissors that needed sharpening from grinding machine installed in Mr Bradleys truck. Wednesday Mr DeMartino would make his presence known as he shouted "Fresh Vegetables...Get your fresh Vegetables" at the top of his lungs from the horse drawn cart only to be out done by Mr Chiello and his melodic voice sing songing ... "Git your Fish Heeere....Git your Fish Heeere..." an hour later as he arrived in his ice covering the back of his station wagon with the catch of the day from the Sheepshead Bay mongers. Thursday was the day that The Bleach Man would deliver his detergents and wine jug bottles of bleach with their screw off metal caps and looped glass handle at its neck. Friday was always my favorite because I knew that there was going to be a wonderful snack sitting in a bowl on my coffee table in the living room as I watched "Voyage to the Bottom of the Sea" at 8P.M. on channel 7...yep Friday was the day "Charles Chips" man deliver pretzel rods in the round clear plastic see through container with a metal lid and Potato Chips In it's distinctive tan and brown metal round container. The Dunkin Donut truck(before there were Dunkin Donut stores) was always a welcome site for us kids on E55th street as we would rush the truck just as we would the Ice Cream Man in the summertime. Then of course there was Mr Duval who worked at Bond Bread and was famous for walking down the block with two huge bags of day old bread and just leaving them on his neighbors stoops. There was also Mr Brakowski who worked at a Butcher shop and was always taking orders to bring meats home from work as he walked down the block heading for the bus stop. I don't think any block did not have someone who had an "Uncle" who provided cigarettes out of the trunk of his car for a discounted price and for some strange reason was always behind a truck when something or "some stuff" fell off it? Most Mothers didn't drive back then and for the most part they didn't have to .Would you like to know why/ Well as long as you asked I will tell you. You see the reason is ..because we lived in a Neighborhood. Let me repeat that ...we live in a Neighborhood, where people looked out for and helped each other and yes we lived in a Neighborhood where small independent businessmen felt safe to ply their trade on our streets My Mom used to say "I am the only person in this house that doesn't drive" She said Dad drove the car and me and my brothers and sisters drove her crazy!!!!

Your Brooklyn

Brooklyn Mothers Know Everything

Growing up in Brooklyn there were always special events that took place that called for my parents to be taken from our homes. That occasion could have been a Wedding, Funeral, Business meetings or God forbid just a night out for them to just enjoy themselves.

On a night that was to be described by any of the stated occasions I previously stated the question that had to be answered could always lead to these five words..." Who will watch the kids?'

You must understand that when such a momentous occasion took place in any Brooklyn home, the optimum choice was always which Grandmother would be called upon to perform the arduous task of watching their very own Grandchildren (Please understand my needed sarcasm ...for I am quite sure you have all witnessed the... "Why don't we ask my Mother" conversation that was sure to be had amongst your parents) That question alone was in my house a growing a bone of contention and often led to more often than not a heated ....oh well ...let's say discussion ..and leave it at that .

It is my belief and I wonder if it was yours as well that sometimes, just to avoid the hurt feelings and the impossible task of making the "Your Mother ...or my Mother" decision. that was without a doubt going to cause irreparable damage no matter what the outcome, there was an alternative that would solve this very delicate dilemma.

I am in my eighth year living in my childhood and cherished Brooklyn home, which made Big brother Michael, twelve and my big sister Eileen ten and my baby sister Maryann five (Brian was still a thought and a notion in the making). I recall the night that my Dad came home from work at the FDNY after a eight to six tour on a Friday night in his best sheepish tone explaining to my Mom that he had forgotten to tell her that the Fire Department was throwing a... wait for it.... "Racket" on this very night.

Well I don't think I have to explain to you the horror that filled my Moms eyes as she heard the news, knowing that she had spent the day from six A.M. cleaning cooking shopping and tending to our untidy brood we called a family ...and now she was called upon to finally have the opportunity to actually go to a place where she could speak, laugh and actually enjoy herself with other adults and especially other women who shared her very same existence? As much as her strength body and mind had reached her exhaustion point, my Mom knew what it meant to my Dad to show off his beautiful bride .. so therefore she summoned her strength from where ....I don't know and in 90 minutes she performed her magic.

I think I might have left out the fact that Dad announced this wonderful news during the Scrambled Eggs and Toast (Stretch Dinner) dinner, being it was a payday and Mom had to make due with what the fridge had to offer before a payday.

So my Dad casually asks... "Do you want me to call my Mother or do you want to call yours to watch the kids?" Mom looks at him and in her calmest voice thinly veiling her (you have no idea how this works "kinda way) "Gene ..you can't call either one of them and because they can't possibly get here within two hours they both live two bus rides away!!!Neither one of my Grandmothers drove....nor did my Mom for that matter)!!

Mom ordered my Dad to go upstairs and shower and shave and to put on his Sportcoat and slacks which were recently purchased from Bonds Clothing Store on Fulton Street for the last wedding they attended almost a year ago...to which he complied and disappeared up the stairs.

Mom knowing that her four children were not going to go unattended and that Dad would not be disappointed to show off his beautiful bride ...as usual found the solution.

As Dad was showering and following Moms orders, my Mom walked out the front door and marched up to the stoop of our neighbors the Barkers and climbed their stoop and promptly knocked on their front door. Mrs Barker (Pat is what what my Mom called her...however I am 58 years old and will always refer to her as Mrs Barker then, now and always) answered the door and said "'Hi Peggy whats up?" Mom explained to her the severity of her situation and the stupidity of the man she married. Mrs Barker smiled and consoled my Mom by telling her she was also married to a man with equal lack of common sense so whatever she had to say she was well prepared for. You see when two Brooklyn women get together all problems seem to just vanish.

Mom returned to our house just as Dad was coming down the stairs looking like a brand new man with his hair all Brylcreemed and smelling of Old Spice. She smiled at him because she knew just how handsome he did look when he was all dressed up and told him to sit down on the couch and not to move even a muscle until she came back downstairs...and upstairs she went. Dad sat in his lounge chair just to show us kids that he was in charge and Mom couldn't tell him where to sit!!!!.....We knew better.

My Mom to me was and still is the most amazing woman I have ever or will ever be blessed enough to be loved by. She started coming down the stairs and after just about just 25 minutes of preparing herself to go out with my Dad, prior to that she had been a woman who got four kids off to school, did three loads of laundry, made sandwiches for lunch for us, iron my Dads uniforms cleaned four bedrooms, vacuumed six rooms and three hallways, cooked dinner and found the minute to rush into the living room because Michael called her to show her how funny Herman Munster looked dressed as a baby on Television. She now descended the stairs with her Bouffant hair-do and her Joyce Leslie Cocktail dress and the scent of Jean Nate' that announced to all of us she ... she was not Audrey Hepburn... she was not Raquel Welsh .... but she was one beautiful Lady...... and she was My Mom....... and my Dads eyes showed more pride than any of ours .

As if their timing was predestined Moms high heel hit the bottom step as a knock came to the front door. I opened the door and there was Sissy Barker(Mrs Barkers oldest daughter) our next door neighbor who was 16 years old and ready to take on the task of babysitting the Leddy Clan. You see back when I was growing up in our beloved Brooklyn, there was no need to have a Nanny or have strangers look after the children in our neighborhood ....all we needed were the generosity our neighbors and their willingness to help each other.

Sissy was so groovy....(yes I said Groovy) She sat and styled my sister Eileen's hair which Eilleen loved because she only really had two brothers to be around so having Sissy there made her incredibly happy. Sissy made sure to check on little Maryann periodically as per my Moms request As for me and my brother Michael ...well lets just say ....I hope Sissy has forgiven us for the little monsters we were to her that night.

When Mom and Dad arrived home that night I guess about two A.M. the house was quiet Sissy was sitting on the couch half asleep after being worn out between Michael and me and Eileens constant and unending questions about why boys are so horrible. Dad walked her next door and thanked Mrs Barker and Sissy went to bed for a well deserved rest.

The only person who was not asleep that night in my house after Dad got back from walking Sissy home was me. Dad closed the front door and didn't really bother to lock it and Mom had already set up a record (33rpm) and the music was playing....Jimmy Roselli crooned and my Mom and Dad danced in the living room....You see that night an 8 year old boy watched two kids who were deeply in love hold each other and sway on my living room floor ....and neither Grandmother had to take two buses to see it....I just laid down at the top of the stairs and peeked through the bannister. That my friends are a true Brooklyn Love story. There were no red carpets, there were no photographers and no flash bulbs going off,,,,,,just a man and a woman with four kids (well three) sleeping upstairs as they danced with each other in their living room in Flatbush.

Your Brooklyn

Brooklyn Football Story

It is a brutally cold Saturday morning in November at Marine Park ..
Perfect weather for playing football in Brooklyn. The frozen hard as a
rock field is crowded with Hurricane Football players, coaches and parents.
There is a game being played for the Midget Championship(10 -12 year
olds) The two teams competing are The Huskies vs The Legionnaires. I
was a Huskie and my Coaches were Mike Stabile(9/11 R.I.P.) and Herbie
Woram.They like the other coaches in the Hurricane Football Program
were volunteers who all worked their regular jobs and yet made time for
us future NFL Hall of Famers. My own Dad was FDNY, a bartender and
part time fence installer. You see we had five kids in our family and Dad
worked those three jobs to make ends meet. Friday nights were the nights
he bartender and would just about be getting home and get two hours sleep
and then off to the fence job.. My Dad hardly made any of my football
games and I understood and I know it hurt him to miss them.

The game was a hard fought one but the score remained tied until
about 3 minutes left in the game. The Legionnaires had the ball on the
Huskies 20 yard line and looked like they were heading for a touchdown.
The Huskies coach turned to a 10 year old player who had very little
playing time that year because of his small size and told him to get on
the field on the next play at the Safety position. The young boy excited at
hearing the news scanned the crowd looking for a special spectator to let
him know he was "going in" but had no luck. The next play arrives and the
boy finds himself in the game and concentrating on what his coach Herb
just instructed him to do..." Don't let anyone get past or behind you!!!". The
opposing Quarterback takes the snap and drops back to pass and lets the
ball go from his hand heading to his team mate who is being covered by

the Huskies new Safety. The boy realizes the ball is heading right to him instead of the Legionnaires receiver!! The ball lands in the nervous hands of that 10 year old and the interception is made. To him he hears no sound, it is as if the world stopped at that moment. He begins to run as fast as his little legs would carry him with the ball clutched under his arm heading for the winning touchdown. There is no opposing player in sight. Along the sidelines a spectator is running step for step with him and screams at the top of his lungs..." Run you little son of a bitch Run!!!". The boy turns his head for just second to see who the crazy man is and naturally slows down. At that moment a sure score was not to be because an opposing player caught up to him and delivered a crunching tackle 10 yards short of the goal line!!!! The ten year old was devastated and thought he failed until his team mates all crowded him with high fives and pats on the back. The Huskies scored on the very next play to win and the championship was theirs. Everyone was saying to that boy "You had the Touchdown easy.. there was no one near you ... how could you not have scored?" Through the crowd of my team mates high fives I saw that crazy man and we locked eyes and smiled at each other He knew why he didn't score and was embarrassed to tell them the reason but at least his team won.

The crazy man was the boys father and the little boy was me. I like all of you love my Dad and I have searched my memories and could not find a more prouder moment spent with him than that look we exchanged when I was tackled short of the goal line. As you can all probably guess I was never drafted to play in the NFL and you will not see my bust in Canton Ohio, yet this Brooklyn Kid would not trade that day for all of that. I love you Dad.

Your Brooklyn

Brooklyn Pride ...And Generosity

There were always two things that were constant as I observed my life growing up in Brooklyn. One was Pride and the other....Generosity.

Now I am pretty sure that I mentioned that my Dad was a New York City Fireman and that he like many men who were fathers and husbands also worked a "Second Job". They worked that "Second Job' because they were brought up believing that it was the "Mans" responsibility to work hard and provide for their families and earn enough to let their wives be able to stay at home and commandeer the family and its daily routines and wellbeing. As archaic as this previous sentence might have sounded, it was a signature of the times and it was prevalent in my home .My Dad for better or worse was and is to this day, pretty much is a "Male Chauvinist Pig", and I know for a fact he will wear that moniker proudly. He will always give a seat to a woman, no matter the age and will always open a door for anyone.

You see that is what I had as a role model, and I still practice those examples to this day.

Men were men and they had Pride, you could be dirt poor or you could be Rockefeller rich...but your pride was providing for your Family no matter what. This I witnessed with every man I encountered growing up in Brooklyn from my Dad to my football coach to my friends Dads, and all the men I knew who lived on my block. Pride....yes Pride ...some believe it to be a curse ...I believe it to be a code of honor, because that's the way my Dad treated it.

I am just entering my ninth year in my beloved Brooklyn as summer was coming to a close and school was rapidly approaching .There is a buzz in my house because my Mom is pregnant with my little brother Brian and we are all excited about this new arrival to our family that is to happen in

February. I was way too young to realize just what the problem was but my Mom was having a little trouble with her pregnancy and was worried. I overheard her saying to my grandmother on the phone that she was a little frightened .Well that's all my Grandma had to hear, she was on the B-41 bus and on her way to our house in Flatbush before my Mom even had a chance to hang up the phone.

It was a Friday and Dad would not be home till 12 that night and it was Payday. My Mom looked into the "fridge" and to her horror we had no food for her to make even a simple dinner for my Grandma to share with us. The front screen door of my house opened and my Mom screamed..... KEVINNNNN ...I immediately drop my stickball bat as if it had just burst into flames in my hands (a broom handle with electrical tape), when Mom called it didn't matter what I was doing I knew to get home and quick. I run up my stoop and into the house I go. My Mom quickly grabbed a pen and wrote out on two pieces of paper...handed them both to me ...one was a list of groceries and the other was a folded piece paper that I was NOT to open and just hand it to Mr. Pete Fiore along with the grocery list at his delicatessen on Ave N and East 56th Street.

I enter Fiore's and stand behind Mrs. Borgia as she is ordering her "cold cuts" from Pete she tells him to slice the cheese not to thick. He completes the order for Mrs. Borgia and thanks her, as she turns to leave she says Hello to me and asks me when I will be seeing her again? Her son Joey and I were pals, so she knew I would see her tomorrow like every other day she was just being nice as always. Pete (Mr. Fiore to me) says "Hi Kevin, what you got there?", referring to the two pieces of paper in my hand. "My Mom said to give them to you" as I reach on my tip toes to hand them to him over his white porcelain adorned glass fronted "cold cut" case. He reads them and says "Give me a couple of minutes" He disappears into the back room. I just stand by the counter looking down at the slatted wooden floor as I push the sawdust into little piles with my feet waiting .Just as promised Mr. Fiore comes out in a couple of minutes and he hands two large brown paper bags to me and instructs me to go straight home ."Tell your Mother I said hello", he says and out the door I go.

Just as I leave Fiores I see the B-41 approaching the bus stop, I walk up to the bus as my Grandma gets off the though the middle double doors that opened magically by themselves. She is holding a green square box with red and white string tied around it making a cross in the middle with the name "College Bakery" on it .We walk together down 55th Street to my house and I hold the door open for her as she enters the house (my Dad says that's what a gentleman does).

We all enjoyed a nice dinner that night with the contents of the two brown bags Mr Fiore gave me. It would appear that everything was fine with my Mom and her pregnancy. I just think she needed to see her Mom and talk to her so she could tell her everything was going to bejust fine because in February I got to meet my little brother and he was perfect Did I forget to say I didn't have to give him (Mr. Fiore) any money? You see between my Dads Pride (who would never take anything on credit) and Mr. Fiores (who would never tell my Dad) Generosity, my Mom knew how to make everything Ok. Dad saved his Pride by never knowing and Mr. Fiore Generosity was rewarded the very next Saturday morning with $8.76 plus two quarters as a Thank You. He of course would never take the two quarters....but the Pinball Machine at Max's candy store right next door sure did!!! Sorry Mom I hope the statute of limitations is up on that that crime.

Brooklyn Pride and Generosity, two things I am generously proud of.

Your Brooklyn

Your First Brooklyn Paycheck

I am quite sure that I have mentioned the fact that in my neighborhood in Brooklyn there were no families that I would have considered to be by monetary standards rich. I believe that only includes monetary rankings because there were so many other things that made us rich beyond the measures of dollars and cents. I have often wondered why it seemed to me that no one's family was hell bent on trying to become" money rich". Maybe it was because being happy and content were the true goals and family meant everything and not just dollars.

Moms and Dads worked and brought home the paycheck, bills were paid, food was provided and if there was anything left after that it was spent wisely. We never went hungry in my neighborhood and we always had warm place with a rooftop and if you struggled... well, we all pitched in to help. Whether it be a meal sent over or a bag of groceries that magically appeared on your stoop overnight or that wonderful phrase that I heard often amongst our neighbors... "Here is a little something til you get back on your feet again"

Itis not to say that we did not wish for more ...because we did, but if we did not get it… it was not the end of the world and we did not stress over it. It was ok that Mr. Tolan had a Pontiac and my Dad drove a Dodge .It was ok that most of our Moms bought us A&P sneakers and some kids had Keds. It was ok when you went to your friend's house and their Mom used store brand mayonnaise when at home your Mom bought Hellmann's. It was ok to wear your brothers and sisters hand me downs (try to tell a kid today they had to do that and watch the reaction) It was ok when the Good Humor Man came and you had to choose from the $.10 cent selection when your best friend that day was allowed to pick from the $.25 cent section. It was ok that Moms on my block would trade clothes for us kids as we grew out of ours. Mrs. Nelson knew that Christopher's would fit me so she would bring a bag down to my Mom.

I will not give you that .... "We didn't have and we did not need it" old line some will say. We wanted to be better off than we were just as much as the next family ...yet it was not an obsession and it was never a label to be tagged on you if you did not. To a kid growing up in Brooklyn the things that we needed to have fun and be happy cost us next to nothing.

Therefore we never knew if we were well off or dirt poor .The majority of us fell right smack dab in the middle. Money was not what controlled our youth, not like when you consider the values of today (if your kid does not have the latest iPhone, they will be ostracized by his peers).

Then something changed when you hit your teens. You see the money coming into your house by the grace of your parents remained the same. However we were no longer just kids and your personal cost of living was rearing its ugly head with its rising cost .We on the other hand were beginning to want and need things that cost more than just having to buy a "Spauldeen"

Girls of the teen entering years were discovering themselves as beautiful young Brooklyn Princesses and were bitten by the fashion bug so they needed to buy new clothes constantly. Boys at the same time were noticing these Brooklyn Princesses that suddenly blossomed and were eager to impress them so they too had to step up their game attire as well. To me personally the prices of good athletic gear (shoulder pads for football, skates for hockey....) was making me yearn for extra money and there was none to be found in my house of 5 kids.

So on the morning of July 15th (my 12th birthday) I like most kids from my neighborhood or my block on their 12th birthday was about to embark on my journey and Rite of Passage into the world of earning a living. Dad and myself jump into his Dodge station wagon and we are off to Lafayette St (downtown Brooklyn) for me to receive my affirmation of manhood ...That's right guys I am getting my ... "WORKING PAPERS!"

I am peddling as fast as my legs would allow with the documentation from the state of New York stating that this 12 year old young man was fit and able to work gripped tightly in my sweaty hand I drop the kick stand of my Royce Sting Ray Bike and enter a storefront on the corner of East 53rd and Ave N .I push the papers across the desk to Mr. Severino. He reads them and says "OK Kid you take E55th from Ave J down to Fillmore Ave

You got that? Now here is a carry bag and your first box of rubber bands are free after this you pay a $1 a box...you start tomorrow"

Itis official I am a working man ...I am an entrepreneur...I am independently wealthy....I am a Long Island Press Paper Delivery Boy!!!

I worked that paper route as if it were a billion dollar business. After School I would race home change from my school uniform rush to the Press office fold and rubber band 54 newspapers and strategically place them into my bag just so they made my flinging them onto the stoops as easy as possible. On the weekends it was up at 7am and finish by 9:00 and race to Marine Park for Hurricane Football Practice. Wearing my brand new shoulder pads (that I paid for at Triangle Sporting Goods on Ralph Ave).

Yes I paid for them with my own money from my hard work. I like every kid in Brooklyn knew that if I really wanted something bad enough our parents would surely not deprive us of it, no matter what sacrifice had to be made, because that's what they did and we knew it was from love.. But God it felt good for the very first time not to have to ask them.

I am sure that each and every one of you reading this has just thought back to the very first purchase you made with money that you earned. Am I right?

Brooklyn offered an array of jobs for kids back then. You must also remember fast food places such as McDonald's and Burger King had not come onto the scene just yet. There Lumber Headquarters, there was Gil Hodges Bowling Alley, The Male Shop, Babysitting, Lenny and Johns Pizzerias, Landis, Pastosas Johns Deli and all the other local businesses that would hire young boys and girls because they knew your parents and because they enjoyed having local kids working in their shops.

You see it was almost like Brooklyn was giving herself a chance to take care of her teenagers and giving our parents a well-deserved break.

I can honestly say that from that very day in that office on East 53rd Street and Ave N, I have worked every day of my life since. Over those years I have earned a lot of money and cashed many a paycheck. I have also made many major purchases in my that time for exorbitant amounts of money compared to that of the amount I handed a man behind the counter at Triangles Sporting Goods in exchange for Spaulding Gladiator shoulder pads. But you see all those purchases between then and now I have to say are mostly doing the same for my family that my parents did for mine, and I am okay with that,because that is what we do for our families. But I will never forget just how fantastic it felt having earned the money for those shoulder pads.

There is just one more thing I must add to this story. Of course a paper boy relied on tips and sometimes there was a bonus ....Thank you Mrs. Berkowitz for the kuegel...I still love it today. Brooklyn like our families always provided for us ....you just had to be willing to earn it from her.

Your Brooklyn

Brooklyn Kids Had To Live Without Computers!!!

There are many places I enjoyed going to as a kid growing up in Brooklyn. I am afraid that one of those places is slowly becoming obsolete. Unfortunately the evolution of technology is taking this place of wonder and making it an archive of the past.

I am sitting at my desk at Mary Queen of Heaven in my 5th grade classroom as Sister Gerald writes our Social Studies assignment on the blackboard. The subject of the assignment is Rubber. She has written on the board the information that she would like all of us to provide her regarding this subject. Such as where it is manufactured, what country produces the most of it, what is the process from plant to finish product and so forth. The very last sentence that she writes as the chalk squeaks on the chalkboard is.... You need to use at least three sources of references and name them in your report.

We all knew what that meant, there would be no playing ball or anything else after school. So at three O'clock the dismissal bell rings and we file out of school and begin our journey home. I come through my front door throw my books on the dining room table and announce to my Mom my homework task. She knows right away where I have to go to complete this assignment. She hands me a dime and a nickel and says to me 'Be careful crossing the avenues and don't worry I will keep a plate warm for you when you get home". Out the door I go and down to the bus stop on Ave N to wait for my old friend "The B-41" to ride me to my destination. With my black and white marble notebook in hand I board the bus drop my dime and nickel into the coin slot and am on my way. We travel along

Flatbush Ave and I am looking at all the stores and people shopping .I know my ride is almost over because I am passing Prospect Park. Then I see it ...it is a building like no other. I pull the cable cord to notify the bus driver that I need to get off. I step to the middle of the bus as it comes to a stop and await the green light above the door to announce that I can open the doors and exit. I stand before this building and look up to the top of these massive steps to the door with huge stone pillars on each side of them being guarded by two ferocious Lion statues. I am pretty sure you all know where I am by now....The Brooklyn Public Library. I climb the steps and enter through those great doors and the noise and bustle of the street behind me disappears as I walk down these hallowed halls .I find my way to the Library Card Catalog and am about to put to work my knowledge of the Dewey Decimal System to work .The cards in the catalog provides me with the location of the books I will need to accomplish my quest .With the tree books that I required located to the tables I am bound. I sit there writing down the information that I needed in complete silence as everyone else for whatever reason they were there for did the same. To me it was totally amazing that with the amount of people in the same building and you could almost hear a pin drop. I have never witnessed this in any other building in my life since.

I loved the Library, yet I fear children in the future will only know it as a reference on an internet page about things from our past. It is by far a simpler way to get information on the internet but It worries me that children will never experience the thrill of finding the one book you need in a building that holds millions of them and most of all the feeling of holding a book in your hands as it feeds you its content and secrets that they hold

Will you miss our Libraries when they are gone?

Your Brooklyn

When the Sun Goes Down in Brooklyn in the Summer.

One of the very best things about Brooklyn summer days, was that Brooklyn summer nights were always sure to follow. The dinner table is cleared, plates, cups, and silverware are washed dried and put away. That was the routine in my house. Without those chores performed by myself and my brothers and sisters, there was no going out to play, period!

I grab my trusty "Spauldeen" and head out the front door leaving the screen swinging as I leap down my stoop and scan my block to see who I can get to play "stoop ball" with me. It was almost as if every family ended their dinner at the same time because within just five minutes every kid on my block was out and ready to play. Itis officially a Brooklyn summer night on my block.

The temperature goes down just a little bit because the sun has set but make no mistake it is a HOT summer night and the humidity made it actually feel hotter. Just as every night when the sun sets the streetlights come to life to announce the night has begun. If this were a school night that streetlight would be telling you to get your butt home, but not on a summer night no sir, this time it meant the fun was just beginning.

Your block is humming with the sounds kids playing and babies being put to bed and our parents sitting on the stoops talking with the neighbors about the news of the day and the things that adults spoke about. Inevitably the sound of a transistor radio being played on someone's stoop could be heard. Whether it was Phil Rizzuto or Ralph Kiner letting us know how our beloved Yankees and Mets were doing or the of the voice of The Chairman of The Board singing "Strangers in the Night" You see our

Moms worked all day in the house with just us kids to talk to and we were rarely inside so to my Mom getting to sit on the stoop with our neighbors and friend (which to me are both the same) was special to her because my Dad worked two jobs, I think she sometimes got lonely and just need to have a little fun with other adults. I think other Moms were the same because they were all laughing and having fun out on their stoops.

Its summer so your curfew has been extended and now it is around 10:30 or maybe even 11:00 you are still out playing in the street and all your friends are hanging out too. You are running around playing maybe "Flashlight Tag" or "Red Light Green Light One Two Three" and then all of a sudden a sound could be heard that makes everyone stop dead in their tracks. It is a sound like no other, it cannot be mistaken for any other sound Itis the most wonderful sound a kid could ever hear...you recognize the melody of the repetitive wordless music It's "'FREEZER FRESH" or "MISTER SOFTEE" !!!!!!

It is as if every kid reacts at once. It is sheer pandemonium we scatter and run for our houses screaming as if our lives depended on it, we begin to scream even three house before our own..." Mom the Mister Softee is here can I have some money?" You reach your house and there is Mom sitting on the stoop with Mrs. Barker, Mrs. Nelson and Mrs. Duval. You are now almost out of breath from the Olympic sprint you just performed to get there... "Mom can I have money for Ice Cream please?"

Your Mom reaches into her "Poccabook" gets out her "Change Purse" counts out .35 cents and you begin the race to see if you can be the first one on line at the truck. I run as fast as my legs would allow only to see Stephanie Barker-Phillips already at the truck window (I don't care what any guy on East 55th street says... Stephanie could run faster than all of us). I stand behind her already sweating from running to the truck, but it is even hotter standing by the humming generator as the heat comes off of it as she gets hers and then I step up and order ...Vanilla in a Sugar Cone with Rainbow Sprinkles!!!!!!Now I know that in my life I have had Ice Cream more times that I wish to admit but it has never tasted any better than it did those hot Brooklyn Nights of my youth. So here is my question... What did you order????

Your Brooklyn

A Brooklyn Rite Of Passage

Growing up in Brooklyn there were a few moments when you knew you were no longer "just a kid". One of them was when you fell in love for the very first time.

Now I have to say when I was a kid the very thought of playing with girls seemed to be a total waste of time. They could not even throw a baseball, they could not catch a football and they didn't know how to skate and hold a hockey stick! So for those reasons I never really had much interest in girls. They would sometimes play "Freeze-Tag" or "I Declare War" and "Ring-0-Livio" on the "Block" but they were too slow and were usually not very good at them. Even sometimes when there was an odd number of us guys to play a ball game we would ask a girl to play just to even out the sides, but you would have to spot the team with her 5runs. Girls? I don't know, who needs them?

Then when I was in 5TH grade and in the last month of the semester in Mary Queen of Heaven ...it happened.

We were told that we were going to have a new student from another school in our class. The door to the classroom opened up and in she walked into the classroom ...and straight into my heart. It seemed like everything was moving in slow motion she took her seat and I could not take my eyes off her. Every one of my friends wanted her to be their girlfriend, but I was, I guess just lucky because she picked me. I can't remember ever being happier and proud and even "cool" at the same time.

We were "Going Out"....which meant I was allowed to hold her hand when walking down the street, which meant I could get to say in my toughest Brooklyn voice... "That's My Girlfriend back off pal" but most of all it meant I got to walk her home when the street lights came on and get to kiss her goodnight at her stoop. It was like magic because after that kiss goodnight because I would feel as if my feet never touched the ground as I walked home and I would begin to count the hours until I would see her again.

Now there is one very important part of "Going Out" that told the world she was mine. It was the ritual for every Brooklyn teenage boy to perform in order to make your relationship solid. So I saved my money and I and found myself standing at the glass counter of Malsons Jewelry store in the Kings Plaza saying "Yes I would like it engraved"....Yep ...you got it ......" "The official symbol of Brooklyn Love"......The Ankle Chain!!!

Oh by the way, one of the other moments when you know you were growing up is unfortunately when your heart gets broken ......you see She "Broke Up" with me before I had the chance to give her "The Ankle Chain".............. Which I still have to this day!

I am happy to share with you that we are best of friends still to this day and had a wonderful laugh about it when I finally told her after 40 years.

I had purchased at least 10 more of them though out my teenage years but none of them were more special than the one I still have in my jewelry box.

So who remembers giving or getting ...The Ankle Chain?

Your Brooklyn

They Only Taste Good When They Are Made In Brooklyn

There are many things that when I look back to my youth that defines solid and unique things that could only be found in Brooklyn. This to me is the quintessential signature item of Brooklyn.

I remember my very first bike ride on East 55th Street, I remember my very first Home Run in Whiffle Ball (It landed on Mrs. DeVito's roof), I remember the first movie I saw without my parents at the Brook Theater on Flatbush and Flatlands Ave .I remember my first kiss on a stoop on East 58th Street from a girl named Katie. You see I can recall most of the special moments in my life growing up in Brooklyn and this is definitely one of them. I am pretty sure that all of you will remember this moment as well because it is something from your past that only Brooklyn people have the pleasure and right to call our own.

Itis a beautiful fall day in our little corner of the world we call home ...Brooklyn. Itis a special day in my house because it is Mom and Dad's Anniversary. It was their 16th Anniversary so that made me ten years old. It is a little after noon and Dad says he is going out to do a little shopping. I ask him if I could tag along with him .You see my Dad worked two sometimes three jobs so there was very little time to be alone with him being one of four kids at that time. He says sure and we are out the door. We walk up to Ave N and head down the Ave .We pass by the shops along the way Yolondas Bakery, Fiores Butcher Shop Henrys Bar., The American Legion Hall, FIilmore Realty and all the many small Mom and Pop shops that lined the Ave and made up our little town. Dad would always wave and say hello to everyone he knew ... and even the people he didn't. My Dad is the friendliest man I know and most people felt the same way about him.

We arrive at the first leg of our shopping expedition which is Austins Pharmacy and Drug Store. We enter and find our way to the Greeting Card Aisle .Dad selects just the right card for his Bride (My Mom) as he has read it and feels that this is the one .We then locate the Candy Aisle and Dad picks out a box of Schraffts Chocolates which is Moms favorites and up to the counter we go to pay. Dad pays asks Mrs. O'Rielly (the cashier) about her family and wishes her well and we are then back on Ave N. We cross the Ave and walk into Cris Florist because Dad knows Mom loves her Roses and he wouldn't dare disappoint, especially not on this day. Card, chocolates and roses in hand and our mission is accomplished and we begin our journey back home. Dad says thanks to me for keeping him company on this little shopping trip. I am so happy because he made me feel like his Pal.

When we reach East 58th and Ave N, tell you what he says "Let's me and you stop in here for a little special treat"...... "Sure sounds great to me" is my reply.

Into the corner Candy Store known as" Ninos" we go. Behind the counter in a crisp stark white t shirt with an apron around his waist is Nino standing behind his fountains looking like the king of his domain. Nino was not a tall man but he had the biggest arms I ever saw aside from Charles Atlas(anyone remember him?) Dad places his order for the two of us as we slide our butts onto one of the red vinyl covered cushioned spinning stools that seemed to defy the laws of physics with its one leg to balance a person of any size as they lined the long marbled formica countertop like metal mushrooms .Nino says to my Dad "You got it" .With the skills of a surgeon Nino begins his concoction ...first the milk... then the soda...then the syrup (chocolate or vanilla)...That's right, you got it... The Brooklyn Egg Cream!!! The most delicious fountain drink ever created ... if made the right way... and Nino was the master in my opinion. I am sure you all have an opinion as to who made the best, but I don't think I ever had a bad one. The oft-cited irony of the egg cream is that it contains neither eggs nor cream. Itis in fact a simple mixture of just three ingredients: milk, seltzer water, and chocolate or vanilla syrup. How it got its improbable name, and was invented in the first place, is the subject of much debate? But one thing is for sure it is a part of Brooklyn as big as any other. We finish our Brooklyn Egg Creams and wipe the froth our mouths with a napkin we got from its metal holder on the counter, Dad lays two quarters down on the counter and we get off our stools to leave and Dad shakes Ninos hand and I am instructed to do the same. On the walk home I thanked my Dad and asks if we could do this again tomorrow? He told me that this day was a treat and to do it every day would ruin its special feeling. I didn't have many days like this with my Dad because like I said his work and four kids, but I will never forget that day

That day I got to not only be my Dads Pal but I had my first Brooklyn Egg Cream and to me that is a day that could not have been any better...... only in Brooklyn .....Only. In. Brooklyn.

Your Brooklyn

Summer Is Officially Here

It's the beginning of summer. School is out all your friends on your block are outside playing Ringolevio, Tag, Hide N-Seek, Stickball, Whiffle Ball, Box Ball, Skully, Stoopball, Freeze Tag, Hit the Penny.... etc...etc.... (name your own game). Someone opens the Johnny Pump and we all go wild. It is official, summer is here! The day begins to give way to dinnertime, and you hear the sound we all seem to dread ... mine was "KEEEEEEVIN TIME FOR DINNNNER"... "OK MOM I'M COMING" was my disappointed reply. Knowing that playtime was over for at least the next hour and a half. You mumble under your breath and head home only to realize that everyone else's Mom is calling them too, so you don't feel so bad..!!! So down dropped the broomsticks with it's black electrical taped crossed in a downward spiral fashion that were created to be a bat.....that was to propel a Spauldeen pink rubber ball as many sewers as your adolescent body was able to project it and hopefully score a run for your team and determine that you ruled the stickball championship of the free world. Down went the plastic handled jump ropes that were sometimes just tied to a silver crossed link fence and told the very confusing story of "Miss Mary Mack ...Mac...Mac...all dressed in black... black... black", pushed aside are the melted crayon bottle caps from the middle of the street that was home to a carved in asphalt playing board just as you were about to hit the other cap for your "Killer Shot" proving your thumb skilled dominance over all the other players on your block....Skelly. The whiffle ball that was just fifteen seconds ago smacked into Mrs. Bauer's Rose garden and to all who ever played whiffle ball in their lives know that ...it's a ground rule double, and it will lay there in wait until dinner is complete. For on my block when dinner was announced by the choir of Mothers calling each and every one of our names, you just stopped whatever you were doing and made your way to your house and hope to be the first one finished with your dinner and after dinner chores and the first to retrieve that ball from Mrs. Bauer's Rose Garden. The first to pick up that stickball bat that has rolled to a stop at the edge of the curb three feet from the sewer grate. There is something just a little bit different on this particular evening, there is just something in the air that confirms this is no ordinary night in Brooklyn. This night holds a very special significance. Of course school has been over for the last week, so that can't be it. The sun has been keeping it's presence known by the longer she held majesty in the Brooklyn sky and the extended the hours of light that was welcomed by all .No as sure as all these things I mentioned are true, there was definitely something else that made thing night just a little bit special. I can tell that I am not alone in feeling this way because I can see it in the eyes of my fellow playmates because there is an aroma that drifts down our block and gives us a hint as to why this night is special.

I like every other kid on my block adhere to the bellowing sound of our Moms voices calling us to suspend our playtime and return to our homes for dinner.

As you approach your house and wave goodbye to your friends you turn down your alleyway and peer into your backyard. The special feeling that this particular night is hinting at is beginning to reveal itself. Your eyes are revealing your suspicions but your nose confirms it, although it may have been over eight months since your smelling senses have experienced this the most wonderful scent God ever created greets you as you head down that alley. The scent is that of charcoal, lighter fluid and heated tin foil............. It's a BAR-B-QUE!!! It is not just any Bar-B-Que....It is the very first Bar -B-Que of the summer which to most of us said...it was officially summer even though the end of school was its first indication. It feels just great to not have to have your dinner in the dining room that has been the natural place for it over the fall and winter and spring months. You are about to eat your dinner without a roof over your head unless you consider the sky a roof, Your view is no longer the four walls that surround your dining room, but the backyards of your neighbors and friends.

Dad stands triumphantly over a 24" round Charcoal Grill (not some lame gas grill) ...his culinary domain. Hot Dogs, Hamburgers, Corn on the Cobb, Macaroni Salad, Potato Salad. The Redwood table and benches are set up and a red and white checkered tablecloth separates the table from the food. Paper plates Tupperware Salt & Pepper shakers and paper Dixie Cups and plastic knives and forks (which means...easy clean up and back to the street pretty quickly). Moms voice can be heard saying "Could someone get the door for me"...as she has her hands full with a hot pot of baked beans (VanDeCamps). We race each other to the backscreen door to be the first to let Mom know that we are there for her and am willing to help wherever we can. As she descends the back stoop and places the pot on a pot holder as not to burn the tablecloth Mom places a ladle in the steaming pot, she then grabs the Tupperware pitcher and spins it's top to open its spout and pour Kool-Aid(Black Cherry was our favorite) into those metal green, purple blue,yellow and orange cups and the Bar-B-Que is officially inaugurated You slide your 10 year old little butt onto the Red And White Checkered Redwood picnic tables bench and claim your spot, your eyes are wide with wonder as they scan the table of summertime food delights. You can see the delight of this anticipated meal does not just belong to you as you notice the look in the eyes of your brothers and sisters. You have this feeling that you are the luckiest kid on the planet and you feel sorry for anyone who does not share this feeling you have. You have waited 8 months for this moment ......You were well aware that there was a very small window of opportunities for a meal such as this. So here is my question ... What food do you put on your plate first?

Your Brooklyn

Chips on the Ball
(Spauldeen) Of Course

The sun rises on a beautiful July mid summer's day in Brooklyn. My brother Michael is the first to make it dressed and downstairs to the kitchen table for Moms breakfast. Eileen - my big sister and myself finish making our beds .race down the stairs with our hands sliding down the bannister making a squeaking noise that could be heard through the house and simultaneously plop ourselves down for breakfast on those avocado colored cushioned vinyl upholstered kitchen chairs with the metal studs that adhered the cushions to its metal frame. The stove, refrigerator and bread box (which actually had the word Bread on it) also bore the Avocado color, making everything match in my Moms kitchen. Even our cookie jar that was a sculptured porcelain round ball of yarn with little kittens attached to it in a playing scene was a shade of green to keep up with the motif. Mom ladled out the scrambled eggs to each of us just as our four slice Proctor & Silex toaster popped out four evenly toasted light brown (the dial setting on the front under the plunger showed you the choices of color toast you preferred) pieces of Taystee Bread stuck their heads from the toaster announcing that they were ready to join the eggs on our plates. Eileen as she always did took it upon herself to butter the toast for all of us, so off comes the top of our Tupperware butter dish(yep, you guessed it Avocado green) and with a butter knife she cut a pat of Imperial Margarine and spread it over our toast and then cut them in half.

Mom asks a pretty blanket question, "So, what are you all up to today?"

Michael is first to answer, he tells Mom that he and "The 55TH Street Bombers" were taking on the 56th Street boys in an all-important

Stickball game for the championship of the free world ......not really but at least bragging rights for that weekend. Eileen says she is going to Barbara Tolan's Backyard to hang out and listen to the new 45s on Linda Brennans new portable phonograph with Stephanie Barker- and Millie Terranova. They would always make up new words to the songs they listen to as they bounced a ball while swing their legs over it in a "My Name is Alice" kinda way...

I tell Mom that they just announced the starting line ups for the All Star Game in baseball to be played Tiger Stadium in Detroit that night, and I wrote down a scorecard (my Dad taught me how to write one at a Met game) in my marble notebook and I was going to play that game with the stoop as my stadium with all its stars in my head waiting their turn to see if they could put one across the street off Tom Seaver the All Star Pitcher.

The morning begins to unfold, Mike Brennan, Tommy (PJ) Joyce, Paul Rasmussen, Mike and Marty McHenry, Glen Nelson and my brother Mike meet the hated rivals at the Ave M side of the Block. Each team with Stickball bats (Broomsticks with black electrical tape) in hand and gloves adorning one of their hands prepare for battle as they eyeball each other.

Ground rules are agreed on after some heated debate and game is about to begin, when someone as someone always would screams out .... "Chips on the Ball". The Block is coming to life with its everyday activities as I looked her up and down before I was to throw the first pitch at my stoop to begin "The Midsummer Classic". Denise Miello and her sister Fran were playing "Hit The Penny" in front of their house on the sidewalk. Down towards the Ave L side of the block a big round circle with dividing lines making it resemble a pizza pie was being drawn in the middle of the street in chalk by the Baxters and the Harrington kids. They were going to play "I Declare War on... every player pick a country and wrote it in chalk in their slice, the person was "up" would bounce the ball in the middle of the circle as hard as they could and scream ...I Declare War on, and if it was your country you had to wait for the ball to come down and if it was not your country you ran as fast as you could to be the furthest from the player who got the ball so it would be harder to hit you with .

At the end of the day Tommy (PJ) Joyce hit one two and a half sewers to secure a win for the boys from 55th Street ...Eileen and her friends came up with a song to bounce a ball to that's lyrics included the names of all the boys on our block that the girls secretly liked....War was declared on Germany repeatedly throughout the day as the ball almost hit the streetlight with each bounce ....Fran and Denise Miello-Lombardo hit that penny so many times

Abraham Lincoln could barely be recognized ...as for me ...well Tom Seaver gave up a Home Run(that landed across the street in The Reda's front yard) to Boog Powell the hated first baseman for the Orioles in the bottom of the ninth with Rod Carew and Tony Coligniaro on base giving the American League another hard fought victory.

You see everyone on My Block had a ball ...I am going to repeat that again....Everyone on My Block had a ball. I want you to think about that for just a moment ....If you look back through this written memory of mine (and yours... just different names you insert) you will find one very special common denominator... Now I am pretty sure that the Family whose name adorned this object never spelled it the way we said it but to me it was and always will be... (come on guys ...have you figured it out yet?)...... Spauldeen...not Spaulding.

Yep it was a little round light pink seamed rubber ball that cost .22 cents and it was the lifeblood of numerous activities that entertained us as we grew up on the streets and Blocks in our beloved Brooklyn

You see we all had a ball and its name was Spauldeen ....and there was always "Chips on the Ball".

Your Brooklyn

Rain Don't Scare Us

I am just finished walking Sky (my canine daughter),we got caught in a torrential down pour. I did not freak out and start running home, I just calmly walked home in the rain!! Motorists driving by and my neighbors looked at me as if I was out of my mind. It got me thinking about growing up in Brooklyn and the rainy days of my youth. Now thinking back I seem to recall the rain never stopping us from doing what we wanted to do. The rain never stopped from playing a stick ball game, the rain never prevented us from going to hang out on the corner or at the park,the rain never stopped us from walking to our friends house and the rain never stopped us from going to the store to "pick up a few things" It seemed to me that when it rained we did not bring our lives to a halt ...We got wet and it did not kill us!! I am not sure if this is just a Brooklyn thing but we were not scared of the rain. So here is my question ...When was the last time you walked in the rain?

Your Brooklyn

Brooklyn "Stretch Meals" Were Delicious

Growing up in my neighborhood in Brooklyn I don't remember a lot of what I would call "Rich' families. For that matter I don't recall a lot of "Poor" families either. Either way I really didn't give it much thought about it because these people be they 'Rich or "Poor" were our neighbors and friends and were really never judged by their wealth. We were all to my recollection just families of hard working people who did their best.

I want to choose my words very carefully here so as not to offend anyone. In my neighborhood and even people I knew back then It was usually the Father who worked at a job let's say "outside the house". I say this in this way because to say Mothers didn't work because they stayed home to "take care of the house and kids" would be a travesty of monumental proportions and I don't know of any "job" harder than being a Mom... On the other hand, I am pretty sure, and I feel safe in saying that the majority of the family unit consisted of Dads as the "Bread winners".

Now in my family I was one of five children, two brothers and two sisters. Dad was a New York City Fireman, which was a great job that my Dad loved but with five kids and a wife to feed, he also worked a second job and even sometimes a third when money got tight.

Dad was paid every two weeks and always on Friday. I always remember how my Mom would be constantly struggling to stretch the grocery budget. She would cut coupons out of the Sunday Daily News and collect 'Plaid Stamps" to redeem for discounts at the A&P. There were times that even with her diligent budgeting and saving, come the end of that second week (payday) sometimes she was broke and what food we had for dinner was in question. Dad being a fireman would often have to work that Friday (payday) so Mom wouldn't be able to go food shopping until at least Saturday morning.

So my Mom would get creative in what was to be our Friday night Dinner. I always thought it was because we were "Poor" .She never made it seem that this dinner was a result of lack of money for food, but she turned it into a treat. Mom would make Eggs and Toast for Dinner!!! To myself and my brothers and sisters it was just so weird to be eating Breakfast for Dinner? So there we sat in the dining room as Mom placed a big bowl of scrambled eggs and a plate of buttered toast slices stacked 6 high on the Dining Room table. The only difference between having this for dinner instead of breakfast was that Mom served Milk to drink instead of Orange Juice.

I had always thought that was just something my Mom did for our family .I grew to realize when I was older that that meal was a product of desperation and "making do" with what was left in the "Fridge" and the "Pantry" .I just knew it was one of those many things that Mom did to keep the family going, whether you wish to call it a job that is up to you. Later on in my life was reluctant to speak about this because I thought we were the only family who did this. I now know this to be not true as I have friends who told me similar stories.

What did your Moms make your family for what I now call...A Stretch Meal?

Your Brooklyn

Christmas Shopping in Downtown Brooklyn

I am not sure if this story of Christmas is exclusive to those of us who grew up in Brooklyn, so feel free to insert your own geographical location to please and adapt to your Christmas memories. I have a feeling that there will be a connection to all who read this regardless. At the very least that it is my hope and Christmas wish for all of you who, especially at this time of the year find the moments to reflect on the past Christmases of our youth and the warmth the season provided to all people no matter what your heritage was or where those memories took place ...mine was in Brooklyn.

I am sitting in Mary Queen of Heaven Elementary School in my slanted wooden top desk with it's carved out groove for my pencil to sit at the top and the metal cave beneath my seat that is home to my textbooks and marble notebooks for each subject. Sister Gerald stands stoic with her black and white habit with her back perfectly perpendicular to the chalkboard scanning my 5th grade classroom as I complete her midterm test. I am confident in the fact that my answer to the last question, I believe it to be Henry Ford who was not only the inventor of the automobile but he is also in fact the architect of the assembly line as we know it today. Henry Ford. D...My final answer .To me at the very moment I lay my test paper upon her desk is the moment my Christmas Season begins. My schoolbag even with the extra burden of ALL my textbooks (Our desks had to be empty for the custodians to thoroughly clean all the classrooms during our break) seemed light as a feather as I ran as fast as my legs would carry me home.

Now mind you Christmas day is actually at least three days away. So as I enter my house my Mom announces that we have to go "downtown 'to do some last minute shopping. You see going "downtown" meant something special to a kid in Brooklyn....it meant traveling on a bus ...in my case ...yep you guessed it The B-41.This so called "last minute "shopping was my Moms way of having us in the store with her as she would be able to hold up that sweater or jacket to you so she could know our proper size. .You see our toys were already secretly purchased but clothes for Christmas in my house was a must and this year I didn't mind because I wanted a Pea Coat just like all the Sailors (and cool kids wore) so I was OK. So off we go, we all climb onto the B-41 at 55th and Ave N take our seat by the windows and wait for the magic we know will soon be within our vision. We turn onto Flatbush Ave and within 15 minutes as we approach Nostrand Ave it starts to appear. The lighted Christmas banners in all their garlanded glory seem to light up Flatbush Ave as if we were traveling down The Canyon of Heros. Each banner every other block was fastened to a telephone pole on the opposite side of the street and was provided the electricity from the local shops and businesses at their own cost as it hung over the avenue giving the bus what seemed to be just enough room to pass below them. They were magnificent as the green red yellow and blue lights spelled out the illuminated messages of the season...Merry Christmas....Jingle Bells.... Happy Holidays....Tis the Season...and so forth. The lights would even blink!!!!!!The garland would answer the lights with their own twinkle and we pass beneath this awesome light display, at the very same time people would be walking along the sidewalks gazing up at the lights just as we were doing from inside the bus. I did not know who there were, I did not know what gifts were in their filled red and white colored paper shopping bags that adorned the names ...Macy's ...Gimbels....Korvettes.....May's... and. ....Alexanders, I did not know who was soon to be the person who would be smiling when they opened them ...but what I did know was that they were as much as what I believed to be Christmas was supposed to be and they played the role of shoppers hustling and bustling to make "the season bright" for the ones they loved.

Mom reaches up and pulls the vinyl wrapped metal cord that stretched around the entire bus.to indicate to the bus driver that this was to be our stop. It seemed everyone on our bus was getting off at the same stop as well because the bell rang at least ten times as we all rose form our hard plastic un-cushioned seats and formed a line to the middle doors as the B-41 came to a halt at Fulton Street.

We exit the bus and find ourselves in a sea of shoppers as far as this ten year old's eyes could see just like ourselves scurrying to accomplish our Christmas shopping at the center of Brooklyn's version of what malls would be to come...... Fulton Street. You must also realize one thing, the reason it was so busy shopping these three days until Christmas was because back in our days we (at least I know my family did) lived from pay check to pay check and the week before Christmas was no different. It seemed as if there were millions of people ...all looking to either find the bus or just trying to find a way out of the what seemed to be a colony of bees looking for the last drop of honey but all holding one of those paper Christmas Shopping Bags with the two corded twined handles trying to navigate through the shoulder to shoulder mass of humanity.

Mom says in her best stem voice "Hold hands and stick together" ...now I know she probably said it in her everyday voice but to me at 10years old I could swear it was the voice of God because I grabbed my sister Eileen's hand with Kung Fu Grip and never let go .Into May's Department Store we go and to me the best part of this trip ia about to happen. I look forward to this moment every year with the same enthusiasm as opening the gifts on Christmas morning.....we head through the multitude of shoppers and as if it were Moses parting the Red Sea ..I can see it ....it is to me the most amazing thing ever...The Escalator!!!

I whisper to Eileen please let go of my hand....I want to do it alone this year... she understands and releases our bond and I lay both my hands on each of the 5 inch wide rubber and leather bound revolving handrails that disappear into the floor as I step onto this oh so intimidating collapsing teeth of steel steps that seem to be able to swallow a kid my size whole. I with all my built up courage step onto the step and brace myself with a grip on each handrail and began my accent to the next floor with my family in front of me and my big brother Michael behind me making sure I was alright.

As we arrived at the top of this magical mechanical Carpet Ride ...a recorded voice announced that we were now on the second floor ...House wares...Cutlery and Kitchen wares. It meant nothing to me ...what I was more interested in was in going back down later!

There were no Mans ...There was no online shopping and there was no 10 level parking garages...there was a bus...there was a department store....

there was an escalator ....and there was a family sharing it together every year.

Christmas Shopping ....Do me a favor everybody....go out and buy someone you love a Christmas Gift......just don't buy it online.....but get it from the second floor of a Department store......and don't forget .....Take the Escalator and grab both handrails ...it's gonna be a great Christmas Season. I know it will be for me just like it was in a small little town I call Brooklyn many years ago!

Your Brooklyn

Hey Who Hit The Number Last Night?

Let me take you back in time for just a short journey. The sun is rising over Brooklyn a new day is about to begin. The ever present aroma of coffee is fills the air up the streets. People are waking from their slumber and the stirrings and every day household sounds fill the homes. I am 10years old and I find myself walking down my street heading to my daily destination to fulfill my morning chore. The place we all meet every morning. I am joined in my task by many others, who seek the same thing I do. They are from all walks of life, housewives, kids like myself, men going off to work and an occasional "Wise Guy" would also be there for the very same reason. Itis something we all can't possibly live without. Itis the lifeblood that connects us to the rest of the world. It would seem to me that we all required the need to be here every day at just about this time. Yet by the end of every day the purpose and end result of our everyday journey to this place, was the genus of all communication and family conversations. It would also give everyone a reason to talk to each other. Itis something that has unfortunately been lost as of recent years and I believe it has weakened the personal bonds and connections that were shared by friends, family and even an occasional stranger, and that saddens me deeply. It only cost a dime but to our way of life it was priceless. It carried a wealth of information that was vital in our everyday lives to all walks of life .There was no escaping the fact that if you did not have one everyday there was a very strong possibility that you would missed out on something that everyone else knew, and that would be unheard of, because we Brooklynites have to be aware and know everything, right?

So there I am walking down my block as I say Good Morning to Mrs. Kennedy as she is in her "house dress" sweeping the front of her house and stoop just like she did every morning." Good Morning Mrs. Kennedy" I say in a sing song kinda way, she replies "be careful crossing the Ave Kevin, make sure you look both ways now", just like she said every morning when we meet. Then as I am passing by the Petrolongo house Mr. Petrolongo is taking in the milk from the" milk box" for his morning coffee and says "How ya doin kid?".... "Just fine Mr. Petrolong", sounding eerily like the Beaver". He says to me "'If you goin around the corner for your Dad Pick one up for me." He reaches into his pocket and flips me a dime from the top of the stoop and I catch it with two hands. He says "The Yanks could use a kid like you with hands like that" I tell him "I want to play for the Dodgers,he looks hard at me and says "Dem bums went to California and left New York high and dry, stick with the Yanks kid, stick with the Yanks."

Now I am almost there as I see people gathered outside and they are striking up a little conversation. I say excuse me to those I step past and enter the store and there it is, the very reason for my daily quest...

How else would we know that the Yankees swept that twilight doubleheader? How else would we know what Boback had on sale today and if the A&P was cheaper? How else would know if Dondi or Brenda Starr or Little Orphan Annie were in deep trouble? How else would we know which horse came in and which just showed, How else could we know what time our favorite cartoon came on the television How else would we know if the Dow Jones took a dive the day before, How else could we know how to not invite someone to our homes without the social etiquettes that Ann Landers make us aware of, How else would we know if someone from outside our neighborhood had past away and where we could go to pay our respects, How else would we know how to plan our fishing trips to Sheepshead Bay until we knew when high and low tide would be. How else would that "Wise Guy" know who hit the number the day before?

I hear the gravelly voice of Joe the Candy Store owner say 'Next' ...I step forward and place the two dimes my Dad and Mr. Petrolongo gave me on the counter and Joe would say..." Just the Newspapers?' My reply was "Yes Sir and my Dad said to say hello". Out the door I go I race home with The Daily News under my arm so Dad could read it with his breakfast. I make sure to look both ways just as Mrs. Kennedy told me to. Mr. Petrolongo is leaning on his "Hurricane" silver linked fence gate with a "P" encircled in the metal topper on his gate I hand him his paper and he says stop by his house later on today his wife Sofia was making Biscotti and I was welcome to as many as I wanted .. I run up my stoop and into the house and straight to the dining room just as Dad is about to sit down with his coffee and breakfast, he gives me a wink and tussles my hair and says" Right on time kiddo."

Have we all said goodbye to the "Newspaper"? It was something I thought I would never live without and now I rarely pick one up.

What I wouldn't give to just have one more time fight with my brothers and sisters over the Sunday Funnies!

Your Brooklyn

Christmas Trees, Seafood Midnight Mass and Foggy Windows

It is a cold night on December 24th 1971 as darkness has just fallen in Brooklyn. We are parked at Utica Ave and Ave N in what was up until three weeks ago a used car lot, but this night it is occupied by Christmas trees looking to be chosen to adorn some families living room. Mom is in the passenger seat of our Plymouth Station Wagon with baby Maryann on her lap (no car seat) after making her selection, as my brother Michael and Sister Eileen and myself are leaning against the fold down door in its rear. We stand there listening to Dad state his case as to why he was willing to pay $6 for a tree that was clearly marked $15.

Money was especially tight this year in my house, so Dad specifically waited 'til Christmas Eve to buy our tree because he knew that he would be able to haggle for a better price. My Dad handed the man $8 and then another $1 for the guy to wrap it and tie it onto the roof of the station wagon.

Dad is now on his back, down on the living room floor under the tree as Mom says just "a little bit to the right" (her very last comment was "a little bit to the left") Ten minutes later after at least twenty "little bit here little bit there's" Dad twists the three silver metal prongs as they piece the trees stem and hold it into place and sturdy in the red and green metal tree stand. Two dining room chairs immediately appear on each side of the tree and Michael and Eileen stand on them as they pass the tree light strands (which took Dad 30 minutes to unravel from the year before and the things he said under his breath as he did it was not real Christmas like) to each other as Mom placed them just so. The bulbs were hung, the bunting (skirt) was placed under the tree and the Nativity scene was placed upon it.

Michael places the Angel on top of the tree and Dad plugs in the lights. Now there is just one thing still missing.....the Tinsel! To me this was the best part of decorating our Christmas tree. We would drape a handful in our left hand and throw the tinsel with our right hands, it seemed like 20 lbs. of it would wind up covering our tree (the tinsel was lead based and had a very heavy feeling as you held it).The tree as always was magnificent as Moms eyes would tear up just a little bit as she looked it over

Itis now just around 10 pm and there was another special happening that would soon be a part of this night. But before we get to that I ask Mom if it was alright if I could go down the block to my friend Eddie Corlonis house for a little bit because he was trying to explain to me something about him getting "seven fishes" for Christmas. Mom says 'OK but you better be back in this house by 11:15" So being an Irish kid I am thinking he got a Fish Tank for Christmas and I was going to see his "seven fishes" swimming around in it. Boy was I surprised when I walked into his house and saw his whole family sitting around the house eating great plates of food .I looked at the fish tank which was already set up (Eddie really did get a tank for Christmas) and noticed it had only two fish in it. Mrs. Corloni made me a plate and handed it to me and said welcome to "The Feast of the Seven Fishes". Now everybody is eating fish and I see only two in the tank.........l am a little nervous and to say the least, a little hesitant to eat what's on the plate! I whispered to Eddie "Are we eating the fish that was in your new fish tank?" Eddie bursts into to hysterical laughter and announces to everyone in the room my question which then they joined in the laughter as well. Mrs. Carloni seeing me standing there confused ran over to me and hugged me as to shield me from the laughter as she yelled at everyone to stop laughing or get out of her house. Armando (Eddies Dad) Sat me down and explained to me about The Feast of the Seven Fishes (I am pretty sure be bit a hole in his upper lip to keep from laughing as he did) as Mrs. Corloni stood behind him scanning the room at her guests to make sure not one of them was laughing at me .God help them if they did!

It's now 11:15 and run down the block back to my house. I can see that all the houses on my block have their Christmas Trees all lit up and decorated in the front window of their homes. Outside were strings of big yellow green red. blue and orange bulbs strung around the windows.

Pictures on plastic molds of Santa's face along with Candy Canes and Dancing Reindeer were taped to the inside window .The inside doors wrapped in festive colors were all open and front storm doors were fogged from the heat inside the homes giving an almost frost like look to anyone passing by.

I come into my house and Mom says go upstairs and get dressed, and by the way "There is a box on your bed you might as well open it tonight"

I fly up the stairs touching every third step I swing around the Bannister pole as I reach the top and enter my bedroom. Laid out on my bed was a Navy Doubled breasted sport coat, a white turtle neck sweater and a tan pair of Bell Bottom slacks. On the floor was a box wrapped in shiny aluminum like paper, I tear it open ...just what I wanted ...all my friends had them......they were the coolest shoes ever ...Chukka Boots.

I feel great because I know I look cool and Lori Cook Satriano will definitely notice me now (I had a crush on her, she didn't know) I was heading out to Midnight Mass. Yes I was 11years old and I was leaving my house at 11:45 by myself (Michael and Eileen went with their own friends and Mom and Dad stayed home to prepare for Christmas morning) I am walking to Church as many of my neighbors doors are opening and they join in the procession at this late night hour. They are wearing new coats and scarfs and hats and feeling wonderful like I am in my Chukka Boots.. I can see the crowd gathered in front of Mary Queen of Heaven Church as I hear and see all my friends and every kid from my neighborhood. All of stood in the back of the over packed Church and sung the hymns and celebrated the birth of Jesus.

Lori did not see me nor did I see her.

As per Moms instructions I went right home after Mass .As I think back to that night, I feel a sense of warmth. I enjoyed the Christmas Tree purchase and decorating, I learned that Italians make the best seafood on this planet from a loving family who lived down the block, I received a wonderful material gift (Chukka Boots) which proved to me that my Mom loved me (the best gift ever)because she made sure that she got them for me and I got to join my neighborhood and stand in the back of a church watching some of the toughest guys I have ever known singing hymns about a child who was born in a manger.

Had Jesus been born in Brooklyn there would have been room for him in every home from Red Hook to Canarsie to Mill Basin to Bensonhurst to Midwood to Flatbush to Georgetown to Marine Park to Gravesend to

Bergen Beach to Flatlands to Dyker Heights to Park Slope to Bedford Stuyvesant to Crown Heights.... he would not have been born in a Manger he would have been welcomed and loved and given whatever we had to make him comfortable. And if he was lucky enough to have been born in Mrs. Corlonis house He would have loved the fish and would have been hugged with loving protecting arms of a woman who looked out for all children, like all Brooklyn Moms.

Merry Christmas Brooklyn

I would just like to take a moment to thank each and every one who have read my stories and have written kind words and shared memories in return .Itis my wish for you and yours to enjoy this wonderful Christmas Season and bask in the love that your families and friends offer you throughout the year. To all my Jewish friends I wish you all a Happy Chanukah and the same blessings
Sincerely
Kevin J. Leddy and Family

Your Brooklyn

Tree Story

I just arrived home from a wonderful Christmas Party. In one piece I might add. My bride Robin and I were honored to be invited to the home of some new found friends. It is my wish to become lifelong friends with. Annie Valentin and Sal Valentin and I hope it is theirs. The house was filled with friends and family who were as gracious as its hosts. Somewhere between the kisses handshakes and greetings I found myself standing in front of their Christmas Tree. I stood before this Tree and realized what I believe to be one of the true meanings of Christmas. You see I have often marveled at my bride Robin for the time,energy and painstaking thoughts she invested every year with our own tree and yet it puzzled me. As I looked upon Sal and Annies tree it all became so clear to me. We don't put these trees up every year to just decorate our homes. It took for me to see someone else's Tree to grasp it.. Annie like Robin sculpture a tree for it to be an annual history of the family who lends its history to. I spent a good amount of time standing in the glow of its lights and with each and every ornament I looked upon I watched this families history unfold before my very eyes. Yes we have our refrigerators to adorn our accomplishments throughout the year with its magnetically fastened statements. Yet a Christmas Tree provides the canvas to paint a picture of our loving and spiritual pride in the blossoming of our families. I will from this moment forth look upon Christmas trees in a different light because the lights if you just see them will catch your eye.........but the ornaments will warm your heart ....let the tree tell you the story!

Your Brooklyn

Brooklyn All Dressed In White

It was a February morning in 1969. This was to be no ordinary Brooklyn winter day .This was the day when Brooklyn was transformed into a place of wonderment to this nine year old kid. I wake up from my sleep at 6 am and crawl to the end of my bed and climb down from the top bunk.. My feet touch the cold linoleum floor but 1 don't feel it because I am wearing my "winter pajamas" with the feet and rubber dimpled bottoms (so to keep from slipping), the house is quiet and I seem to be the first one awake as I head downstairs. I always loved being the first one up in my house because with five kids in my family the house was always filled with sounds and voices and commotion so the sounds of silence at that hour was always a special feeling for me and my house. I loved that house.

On this morning however all I could think about was opening the front door to see IT. My friends were all excited about IT, our parents were all talking about IT and the preparations that had to be taken. Even the television spoke of warnings about IT, and this morning IT was here.

I open my front door and I try to wipe the sleep from my eyes because I am not sure what exactly it is that I am seeing because the glass on the storm door is completely white. I jump onto the love seat which is directly under the "picture window" of our living room, standing on the love seat I open the curtains ...and there IT was ....The Blizzard!!!

It was truly an amazing sight, there was still a darkness that had not given into morning yet, and when I look at the street light in front of my house I could see the snow coming down with the help of the wind it seemed to be falling sideways. The cars that were parked on East 55th Street were completely covered and barely visible but the shapes of the roofs of them were unmistakable. I jump down from the love seat and run to the dining room window which offered a view of the "alley way ", I look out to see that the snow was up to the window of the Barkers dining room directly across the "alley way". I then race through the kitchen into the pantry and open the back door that led to my backyard, the snow because of the way the wind hit our backyard had not completely blocked the door from opening, but I had to push that storm door real hard. I opened it and stepped into the space that the door opening created by pushing the snow .As I stand in that snowless little arc on my back stoop I see something that lets me know what a Blizzard is, or should I say that I can't see something that tells me what a Blizzard is? Our 4 ft aluminum sided winterized pool with its plastic winter cover and a big balloon under its cover pool is gone!!!!!!I know it's under that snow somewhere but I can't see it... so this is a Blizzard.

I close the door and step back into the kitchen and find myself eye to eye with my Mom as she is already starting to prepare breakfast, we held a look for a moment .My Mom looked extra beautiful to me these days because she was nine months pregnant with my baby brother Brian. She could see the overwhelming excitement just by looking into my eyes and just smiled at me and said "What are you waiting for? Run upstairs and get dressed... and make sure you put on your "Long Johns" it's really cold out there in snow like this". As quiet as I had gone down those stairs before was equal to the amount of noise I made running up them, as I hit every step the sounds woke up the rest of my family .

Then to my brother and sisters the race was on...let's see who can get dressed and downstairs first? Although I was the first up I was dead last getting downstairs...I forgot to put on my "long Johns" and had to go back.

Mom yells "No one is going anywhere without having breakfast first" So we all sit down for our Quaker Oat Meal (Out of the cylinder shaped container with that old man with the long white hair), I even forgot to put sugar on my oatmeal because all I could think about was jumping off my back stoop and into that white magic. Morn has already laid out our boots gloves scarves and Jackets, but to me the coolest was my wool hat that rolled down over my face with holes for my eyes nose and mouth, it almost made me feel like a masked superhero. OK I step outside the back door and from the top step I throw my body with total abandonment off it and land with a swoosh sound as I plunged down into the snow and my brother Michael and sister Eileen followed .We made snow Angels played and rolled around throwing snowballs at each other for what seemed to be an eternity, it was the best times I recall with them because we were not just family ...we were friends.

Then Dad steps out to join us and announces that we need to get to shoveling, I did not think about it at the time but he knew we needed to get a path from the house to the car and the car cleared because there just might be a trip to the hospital in the very near future!

When we shoveled our way to the front of the house from the backyard I looked up and down the street only to see almost every family out there doing the same as mine. Everyone was so bundled up and the snow was falling so hard that the only way you knew who was who was by them standing in front of their houses. We all waved and screamed hellos at the top of our lungs .The snow was being handled by an army of men and children as the sidewalks and stoops were now visible. Then as if they planned it, it seemed that all the Dads collectively said... "Alright you kids go play I will shovel the rest" .That to me was why I love my Dad so much... he knew ...he just knew. And then all at once kids dropped their shovels and ran into the middle the street screaming and yelling and jumping on each and falling down in the snow. We all began throwing snowballs at each other and some of us built a fort out of snow for defense. Paradise could be found on a snow covered Brooklyn day on East 55TH St. it was freakin awesome!!!

It is now about 12 noon and the Morns call us kids back in for some lunch. We all come through the pantry and remove our snow covered clothing as Morn takes each piece and lays them on the radiator to diy .The kitchen table presents a cup of Campbell's Tomato soup and a grilled cheese sandwich for each of us,.... ya just gotta love Mom!. The warm house feels good but I can't wait to get back out into the snow and cold. Back out we go, equipped with a fresh diy set of gloves and a diy jacket that was laying a top the furnace in the basement as we ate lunch. My brother Michael and the older kids on the block had an idea for even more snow adventures. So about 20 kids from my block walked down Ave L to Ralph Ave to the Georgetown Shopping Center. The parking lot was plowed and the mountains of snow they created was incredible. We played King of the Hill on top of these 30ft white mountains for a while and then we ran to Hills Super Market to get cardboard boxes and we used them as our sleds to fly down those mountains like the bobsleds on ABC's Wide World of Sports until it got dark. Then we all went home for dinner.

We relived the day as we all sat around the dinner table at my house. Michael informs me that after dinner we are going out again but what we are going to do, we can't tell Morn and especially not Dad. Dinner is over and Mom knows how bad we want to be back out in the snow with our friends she gives us all a look and says "My treat tonight I will take care of the dishes and your chores now hurry up and be back in this house by 9 O'clock." Thanks again Mom. Michael and his friends take me along as we walk to E56TH St and Ave M and there are already about 15guys there. So we are all just standing there doing nothing and I am looking at Michael like "This is what I can't tell Mom or Dad?" "Just wait" he says Then a car pulls up to the comer and stops for the stop sign. Michael grabs me and pulls me down behind the car and says "Duck down behind the car keep your ass down and your knees up and grab onto the bumper"...It was the coolest ride I ever took ...the car took off ..I kept my ass down ...and kept my knees up ...and I held onto the bumper and I "Skitched" all the way down to Ave N.

You see we did not have the Ski Mobiles at the Pocono Mountains, We did not skiing at Great Gorge, We didn't have Bobsledding in Lake Placid. But what we DID have was a backyard snowmen, Snow Angels, shovels, stoops, the street snowballs, and forts to throw them from we bad mountains made from snow plows, we bad cardboard boxes to slide down those mountains and we had SKITCHING!!!

To me Brooklyn was the best Winter Resort that was ever created because, it was created by us ....not for us!

There have been many Blizzards since but to me that one was IT

Your Brooklyn

I'll always love my Mama ...she's my favorite girl....

This was The Leddy Castle in the Kingdom
of Brooklyn 1391 East 55th St

The new arrival (L to R) Michael Me Eileen

169 Congress St....It is really hard to look cool when
you are dressed like this! Thanks Mom

It seemed like every house in Brooklyn had this picture in their house (L TO R)Maryann Me Eileen Michael

Alright Mom please take the picture already....
(L to R)Me Eileen Michael Brian Maryann

So Gene Leddy asks Peggy Cronin for a date
and the Brooklyn Love Affair begins

Two Brooklyn Kids make it official ...Mom and Dads wedding

Brians Communion (L to R) Maryann Grandma Cronin Dad
Uncle Jack Cronin Aunt Helen Ward Me and Brian

Easter Sunday in Brooklyn were always so fashionable (L to R)
Eileen Stephanie Barker Theresa Rasmussen and Maryann

The three greatest women in this Brooklyn Kids life (L to R) Peggy
Leddy (Mom) Mary Cronin (Grandma) Catherine Leddy (Nana)

Dressed for a Friday night in Brooklyn ..just going "Nowhere"

Me and My Big Brother Michael....Michael Brooklyn was
a rough place to grow up in sometimes, but when your Big
Brother is one of the toughest guys in the Neighborhood
It was a little easier Thanks Mike I Love You

Eileen and Tony Viviano Another Brooklyn Love Story. Eileen when I needed to talk you were always there to listen, when I cried it was your shoulders that caught my tears Thank you Eileen I Love You

Maryann and my Son Nicholas. Maryann I could spend my whole life searching this planet for someone with a kinder and more caring heart. I know I will never find them. Your greatest gift is your ability to give of yourself to anyone you think needs. I am so glad I am one them. Maryann Thank You I Love You

Brian and Nicholas Brian you are my younger brother and yet I feel
I have looked up to a good part of my life. You are truly what is best
about our family. You Love You Care You Help and you never judge.
There is no better man on this planet. Thank You Brian I Love You

Crazy Uncle Mike and my just as crazy son Nicholas Two tough Guys

Me My Nephew Michael Leddy and My son Nicholas
Leddy. The next generation of Brooklyn Leddys

My Wedding Day (L to R) Theresa Leddy Maryann Leddy Brian Leddy Eileen Viviano (in hat) Me and My Bride Robin Nicholas Leddy and Genna Viviano

This is the girl who honors me everyday of my life by
being My Bride and the most wonderful Mother to our
children Garrett and Jacqueline Robin I love you.

Garret James Leddy preparing to lead Saint Anthonys Pipe Band
down 5th Ave on Saint Patricks Day I have never been prouder in
my life. Garrett I marvel at your dedication and determination
in everything you put your mind to in your life I really admire
you son and that will never change. Garrett I Love You

Nicholas " Doc" You are my first great accomplishment in
my life. I am awed by your intellect and complicated mind
but son I have to say the one thing I absolutely love about
you is that You can make me laugh. I so really enjoy you.
Nicholas I Love You ..... You Little Shit (I couldn't resist)

Jacqueline Taylor you are my most amazing Masterpiece. You have grown up to be an incredible young woman and I enjoyed each and every moment watching it take place. You will forever be My Little Girl" Never forget what I whisper into your ear every night when I check to see if you are asleep. " You are the most beautiful little girl in the whole wide world and your Mommy and Daddy love you very much" Jacqueline ..I Love You

This is 169 Congress Street in Brooklyn ...This is where my story began

EVERETT SCOTT

Boobie I am living a good life ....but I often think how much better
it would be sharing it with you. I never forgot you Brother

Brooklyn Dating Rituals

I am not sure of just how many of us growing up in Brooklyn will have shared this experience with me. I just hope that a few will have remembered this with the same warm feeling I get when reminiscing about dating in Brooklyn.

Dating while growing up in Brooklyn provided a full menu of destinations and venues .The choice was often made by just the kind of night you wished it to be.

Going out to a movie was a constant and reliable event, that provided alone time with your date. However it generally consisted of two people just sitting together with their attention locked in on the film being played,while in some cases intimacy was achieved with a sporadic "make out session" but with very little to none as for as conversations went .

Going to the clubs and dancing was another great night out .The Discos was great because while you were on your date you got to meet up with your group of friends and hang out and share some stories and laughter as well. Between the loud music and being in a group it really left little room for two people to just enjoy each other and talk.

I would be remiss if I didn't bring up double dating. It was usually the people who were your best friends, be it her best friend and her boyfriend, or it was my best friend and his girlfriend. Now I don't know about you but to me it seemed that when double dating, I spent most of the evening talking more to my male counterpart than I did with my own date .She on the other hand did the same with new found girlfriend. So once again the night did not allow the luxury of just being able to enjoy one others company without distractions and other people.

Now one would think that going out to dinner was a great venue for that one on one personal date that provided you the avenue for intimate conversation and to some extent I agree.

However if you really think about it the lion's share of the time spent at a restaurant is consumed by the playful debate as to what to order and then the very act of eating which hinders conversation because Mom always said ... "Never speak with a mouth full" Therefore when you think about it there is actually very limited time for conversation even when it is just the two of you sitting at the table.

There was to me one place that provided an atmosphere that was conducive to just the right date for two people to really 1llax and enjoy a wonderfully intimate conversation with privacy. It was a dimly lit rather large room with mostly booths and tables for two. There was always a person playing soft music while playing a guitar and the menu was limited to Grapes, Fondue and of course "Wine and Cheese."

I felt very comfortable there with our faces lightly illuminated by the candle that adorned the center of the tablet and looked into each other's eyes .We spoke in low tones to insure that our private conversation stayed just that....private.as did all the other couples that shared the room with you, even though it was totally unnecessary. Because while looking around the room you would notice that all the other couples were not interested in your conversation because they were deep in their own... A Perfect Date!

There were not many of them but to me The Wine and Cheese" places were almost the perfect location for a date. I often think about those nights and the girls who shared them with me and thought if there was a "Wine and Cheese" place around today how cool it would be take my wife just for a date and some one on one 'We Time."

Mine was "The Wine and Cheese" ...what was your favorite date spot?

Your Brooklyn

We Are from Brooklyn
Don't Tell Us We Can't

January 12th 1969 was just another Sunday in my beloved Brooklyn. Or so I thought. We all got up at 7AM and got dressed for Mass. Mary Queen of Heavens 9 O'clock mass was the Children's Mass. So at my house my brothers and sisters all took turns waiting at the bathroom door for our family member to wash up brush their teeth and then come out.

Eileen Leddy- Vivia no at the time was 11years old and took the longest because she knew that this guy named Gregg Chercione who had a crush on her would be there so she took extra time to make sure his crush on her would not go unnoticed .With our teeth brushed and relatively clean bodies due to the baths or showers we took the night before, we presented ourselves to Mom for hair grooming and final inspection. Mom combed and or brushed our hair and then meticulously looked over our hands and necks. Necks cleaned and no dirt under our fingernails ...we were ready for church and the saving of our souls.

Farther McNamara presided over the 9 O'clock mass as he was our Parish Pastor and always made it a point to be serving that particular Mass because it was also known as the Children's Mass.

As always we sung our hymns and prayed for the helpless and the poor, we were reminded to pray for all other denominations and of course the sick and recently departed and all the souls of the faithfully departed. We would line the alter and receive communion, return to our pews bow our heads while kneeling on the flip down "kneelers" and pray with all our hearts for our loved ones and the less fortunate of the world .Mass was almost over when Fr McNamara asked all of us to join him in a prayer for a young man from Beaver Falls Pennsylvania who just two years after graduating from the University of Alabama and now the quarterback of The New York Jets to achieve success in his game this day ...if indeed it was the will of God.

Arriving back home that Sunday morning, Dad would be in the kitchen preparing breakfast (he always did that every Sunday to give my Mom a little break)...so the smell of eggs and bacon filled our home. The best was the special potatoes he made.....thin as a communion wafer was the way he would prepare that potato slice fried in butter. It was his specialty at his Firehouse when he cooked for his fellow FDNY mates and he carried that tradition into our home every Sunday .We all took off our coats as fast as we could and where they landed was of no interest to us as long as we got the first batch of Dads special breakfast potatoes. We knew one thing was for sure... that if those jackets where they landed did not find themselves on a hanger and in our closet after we finished breakfast...we would have Mom to deal with. Needless to say they never stayed where they landed and all found their proper resting place in our closets!!!

It was not just my house but every house on my block and I am pretty sure every house in Brooklyn was abuzzed with the thought of a team that represented Brooklyn and all of New York State was playing for the Championship of the Football World. The rest of our nation was giving our team a slim to no chance in hell of winning and to be quite honest scoffed at us for believing they actually could. But what did they know...they were not from Brooklyn and couldn't possibly know the faith we had, no matter what the odds were against us. That young man from Beaver Falls Pennsylvania in good old Brooklyn fashion when asked by a newspaper reporter(there was no ESPN then) if he thought that his team, a 19 point underdog had ANY chance of beating the mighty Baltimore Colts ....he answered ... like any Brooklynite would ....." We will WIN....I guarantee it"

You see in the Brooklyn I grew up in there was always discussions and debates and downright heated arguments on everything from religion to politics to the proper way to sweep the 12ft sidewalk in front of our houses. However it seemed that almost everyone I knew seemed to be in agreement with this brash bragging kid we knew as Joe Willie Namath who was a Brooklynite for the day, and on that Sunday afternoon in Miami Florida January 12th 1969 he held in his skilled hands the pride of not only his New York Jets, but of the entire state of New York ...but especially my beloved Brooklyn .You gotta understand one thing we love an underdog ....we love a fight....and most of all we love to prove anyone wrong who don't agree with us...it's just who we are. We are Brooklynites!!!

Mom and Pop stores that lined our Avenues and Streets closed early and the streets that were usually lined with cars on every other given Sunday were eerily void of its normal traffic, the streets that were always inhabited by kids playing a variety of sports and games were desolate. Everyone was being held captive in our homes by the chance of seeing history being rewritten

It was Super Bowl III and my beloved Brooklyn had a horse in this race "The New York Jets, so we all found ourselves in our living rooms watching our black and white RCA, Zenith, Philco or Motorola Television console sets to witness this national event!

We all sat mesmerized as we watched that kid from Beaver Falls lead our team to victory and cheered and jumped up and down on the very furniture that on any other day would surely be like signing your own death certificate if Mom saw you! We took the same pride of our team in our hearts, as much as David did when he slew the Philistine Goliath.

Brooklyn rejoiced, we ran into the streets banging pots and pans ...fireworks were exploding in the cold January night's sky, something that was normally reserved for the 4th of July.

Neighbors ran into the streets and hugged each other and embraced (the same people who argued over how to sweep the sidewalks) to affirm that they too had witnessed this unlikely triumph

We once again had a Champion ....not since The Brooklyn Dodgers left us with a gaping wound in our hearts had we collectively rallied together as one in a victory we called our own. The New York Jets of 1969 went down in history as the first American Football League Team to defeat the mighty and heralded National Football League in spite of the popular opinion of the rest of our United States. To the so called inferiority of that team who held the hearts and hopes of me and my fellow Brooklynites ...They shook the world and the very heavens. In my opinion that kid from Beaver Falls was exactly what Brooklyn was and is all about......You tell us we can't...we say we will.....You tell us it ain't possible...We show you how....You say "No Way" and we will shove it down your throats.

You can ask any one from Brooklyn a question about any subject on this planet and you will get a million different answers, But ask any one of them who was the guy who stood up in Brooklyn fashion and told the sports world where to go........They will unanimously answer ... Joe Willie Namath ....!guarantee it !!!!!

He may have been from Beaver Falls PA But with the "stones" he showed that day ...he was Brooklyn ...all the way!!!

Your Brooklyn

A Brooklyn Saint Patrick's Day

It is a day in my family and quite a few other families day that we all look forward to. It is a day of celebration and unity. At least that is the way I remember this annual event that took place in my Brooklyn.

It is March 16th and at my house and many other homes across Brooklyn spanning from Bay Ridge to Bensonhurst, From Flatbush to Marine Park From Sheepshead Bay to Gravesend, From Canarsie to Brownsville, From Park Slope to Red Hook, From Georgetown to Mill Basin and Bergen Beach From Williamsburg to Greenpoint and so on. You see tomorrow was not to be just any other day in my beloved Brooklyn. It was to be a special to be shared by all. My Mom that night, upon inspecting the results of mine and my brothers and sisters nightly chores has found them satisfactory release each one of us to find our designated places to begin our homework assignments for the Dominicans Nuns of Mary Queen of Heaven to inspect and critique our efforts.

Mom goes to the pantry closet and removes the ironing board and with nothing less than a Magicians expertise she creates an "X' with a board laying flat over its top, that still today has not been improved on. She then goes to the "utility closet" and removes her Sunbeam Steam Iron and places it on top of that board with the magical "X" that supports it. Plugged in to the wall socket Mom goes into the kitchen and returns with what looks to be a small measuring cup and fills the Iron with the water that it contains for to create the steam that will be required to achieve perfection. She proceeds to to climb the stairs and enters her bedroom, opens the closet and removes a suit from it and descends back down the stairs to the living room where the Iron now filled with water and ready to perform its said task.

Mom removes the navy blue dress uniform pants and begins to prepare this garment for my Dad to wear the following day. My Mom spent uncounted hours over that Ironing Board, but never did she perform that task with more loving and meticulous dedication. This was no ordinary suit she was preparing ..no sir ...this was my Dads New York City Fire Departments dress blues! There was a strong possibility that the man she loved and cared for.... might ...just might.... be singled out by Jack McCarthy on Channel 11 and she would be damned if he did not look just so. God forbid anyone should see him and notice a wrinkle in his pants on their 12" black and white screen, surely she would be ostracized by every woman who attended church that following Sunday. Now we Irish have never been known for our culinary prowess (I am pretty sure the Italians have mastered that art)yet I never looked more forward to any meal throughout the year.

Mom having now completed the pressing of Dads uniform (and I swear you it could cut a piece of loose leaf paper with the crease she created in those pants) and feeling quite proud. She began the process of prepping for the nexts days feast to follow. Carrots were peeled and sliced, the potatoes were peeled and quartered and the cabbage was soaking in salted water and the main attraction was on a platter in the refrigerator...the long annually awaited.....Corned Beef!!

Dad arrived home at just about 5:15 A.M. because not only did he work a 9-6 shift at the FDNY, he also worked a second job as a bartender at a bar in Staten Island called C.J.s on Cebra Ave.. He climbed into bed for the two and a half hour sleep he rightly earned and at 8:15 he was in the shower and by 8:30 Mom was getting him dressed. My brothers and sisters were just about to leave for school at Mary Queen of Heaven as my Dad walked down the stairs. Now I don't know who you call your Heros in your life but to us as we stood in the living watching him walk down the stairs in his FDNY dress uniform...well there was no movie star, there was no ball player or even an astronaut who could hold a candle to him.... he was our Hero! And we got to call him Dad.

Dad was off to march down 5th Ave and we were off to school. As I walked down E55th St. I could not help but notice that in each and every window on my block there was scotched taped green emblems and cartooned characters, like Leprechauns or Pots of Gold and numerous Shamrocks. Yet the funniest thing was they hung in the windows of the Duval family who I knew to be French and they hung inn the Spinellis window who I knew to be Italian and they hung in the Nelsons window who I knew to be Swedish and of course they hung inn the windows of the McHenrys and the Murphys and the McNamaras but that was expected.

You see in my beloved Brooklyn when I was growing up we acknowledged and celebrated for and with each other and we celebrated together. It was a day that gave everyone an opportunity to just be people enjoying an event without having to identify who you were ...we were all IRISH that day

Well do I really need now to tell you it is Saint Patrick's Day....I don't think so at this point. What I do need to tell you was that unbeknownst to everyone on the planet that day ..was that my Dad wore a green yarmulka under his uniform hat and as he passed The Cardinal at Saint Patrick's Cathedral he tipped his hat and revealed a kelly green yarmulka which drew shock and a little smile from the Cardinal. My Dad did it in in honor of a fellow fireman who was wounded two nights prior in a three alarm blaze...his name was Howie Cohen and my Dad wanted to honor him that day at the parade.

I like most kids on my block that day rushed home to see the end of the parade on WPIX Channel 11 because we all knew someone who was marching in the parade and had a small hope of seeing them on T.V.. To this day if you ask me if I saw my Dad that day I will answer you ...yes..did I ? probably not...but who I know that I definitely saw heroes and everyday people enjoying a little happiness for the hard work they so unselfishly performed the other 363 days a year.

Dad by the grace of God makes it home after the parade and the windows are fogged from the boiling Corned beef and cabbage. We all wait for Dad to complete serving himself(Dad never served himself until he saw our plates full) Michael said Grace and we all began eating. Dad told us of how there were a million people at the parade maybe one day we could march with him. Supper was as expected just wonderfully delicious thanks to Mom. Us kids did the dishes so Mom and Dad could enjoy a wee bit of the Poteen (Booze for all you non Irish) together and it was wonderful to see them embrace and laugh.

Well tomorrow will be Dads 60th year marching down 5TH Ave and he will be accompanied by his Great GrandChildren and his chest will be swollen with pride.. I am proud of my heritage just as you are all proud of yours and being from Brooklyn I got to experience alot of different ethnic traditions and customs and I just only wish my children could do the same.

My point is this, in my Brooklyn it never really much mattered who or what you were ...for me I was a Mic others were Spics and Pollocks and Wops and Hebes but not this day my friends ..no not this day ...this day you were all Mics. Yes my friends you were and are all Irish on this day ...and I for one am damn proud to share it with you .....after all when it really comes down to it........We are Brooklynites ...and we celebrate with each other.Happy Saint Patrick's Day to all my fellow Brooklynites.....because I am as proud to be Irish as I am to be one of youse.

Your Brooklyn

Nothing for Nothing

My Dad as long as I could remember always worked two sometimes three jobs. He said to his children he didn't mind working as long as we understood why. You see my Dad didn't have a Dad so he was raised by his Mother (My Nana) whom had to work as a waitress all her life to provide for him and his sister (My Aunt Eileen). He was often left home alone and swore that his kids would never have to be without a parent at home all the time. So he worked as much as he could to allow my Mom to always be there for us. He told us life could be really cruel and miserable if you were not willing to work for what you wanted .

My Mother washed our clothes, made or meals cleaned our homes and wiped away our snotty noses and our tears and applied band aids when needed while cooking,cleaning making us aware of the softer side of life as opposed to the harsh reality our Dads portrayed .

We as children were respectful of our elders, we studied hard at school,we cleaned our rooms and made our beds, we washed our hands before dinner and we never ...ever ...ever called an adult by their first name!

So here we are ...it is Christmas mourning ... the wrapping paper is being ripped from each and every gift my Mom so painstakingly wrapped with its ribbons and bows and the squeals of delight can be heard from each of our surrounding Boroughs .....that intern wakes my Dad after just arriving home from work no less than three hours ago. He makes his way to the middle of the banister stairway that ends in our living room. He stops at the "landing" (three steps above the living room floor) nods his head towards a large box signalling Michael to give the box to Mom.

To this day I know in my heart of hearts his look was meant to attract my older brother Michael's attention but I just by chance turned my head at that exact time and read my Dads instructions. I raced to a shabbily wrapped large box that on the snowflaked adorned gift tag read .... "Peg-O -My-Heart"(My Moms name was (Peggy) and below read ..... "Love Gene" I Rushed right up to Mom and jumped up and down within six inches of her face like an child even though I was Eleven years old to let her know the urgency of opening this box next. She realized without letting us know her disappointment...for indeed she knew it was not the Polaroid Instamatic Camera she anticipated. It was a wonderful 60% poly 40% cotton full length belted wrap around robe. Dad insisted that she put in on right away.. and Mom complied. In the pocket only known to my Dad and God was a a Polaroid Instamatic with color picture abilities. I have seen the look of happiness in my life on the faces of many people and yet to this day none will ever match the vision i witnessed in my living room on December 25th in 1971 I am pretty sure I would still to this day be standing side by side with my brother and sisters in front of that seven foot Fir Tree posing endlessly for my Mom as she took pictures

My Dad got up earlier than he wanted and was able to make my Mom feel special because he worked hard and busted his ass

My Mom got the camera she wanted because she constantly cared for and attended each and every need of our family and was able to show actual proof of the amazing children she thought us to be

My brothers and sisters got all the gifts we wanted because we did our chores and we achieved good marks at school and most of all respected our elders

My friends,,,,,you see whether you realize it or not ...we all earned our gifts.......... because as we all know ...When you are from Brooklyn,,,, "You never get nothing for nothing"

Merry Christmas Brooklyn....not for nothing"

Your Brooklyn

A Magic Kingdom in Every Brooklyn Neighborhood

There was always something special about Saturdays growing up as a kid in Brooklyn. You see during the school year when you came home after school it was generally 3 O'clock which did not leave a kid with much time to play because dinner always scheduled for somewhere between 5 and 6 O'clock in mostly everyone's house. Not to mention that as winter neared it stole the sun from us as early as 5 O'clock making the time for playing even shorter.

Inevitably the call from our Moms signaling it was dinner time could be heard like the Ladies choir at church as each Mom would seem to sing the names of her child or in most cases children, with an almost musical like rehearsal. My Mom had five of us so as she stood on our Stoop with the storm door half open belting out our names at the highest octave she could muster, it was a wonder she had a voice by the end of the week? So Monday through Friday on my block that was the Daily ritual. Don't get me wrong we were able to squeeze as much fun out of those two and a half hours that were humanly possible yet looking forward to Saturday was always on our minds all week long.

Saturday morning is finally here, instead of moaning and groaning to your Mom about being tired and that you did not want go to school, you jump out of bed without having to be woken up. You get dressed in your room and down the stairs we go. I find myself in the kitchen grabbing a bowl from the cabinet and a spoon from the silverware drawer and Frosted Flakes are soon to follow because "Theeeeere Greaaattt", says Tony the Tiger on the front of the box. I walked into the living room ever so slowly balancing that cereal and milk filled bowl as if it were a ticking time bomb one gingerly step at a time so as not to let it spill on Moms floors. I place the mornings culinary delight on "The Coffee Table", I turn on the television and wait for it to "warm up", I kneel down in front of the T.V. and begin to eat my bowl of sugary energy, Bugs Bunny and The Road Runner make their appearance so that makes it official ...It's Saturday

Yep it's Saturday,into the sink goes the bowl and spoon and with my weekly chores complete(which is a story for another day) I tell my Mom I am going to be leaving now and her response is "You just make sure you are home for dinner on time Mister". Yep it's Saturday and it is all mine, and I know exactly where I am going to spend it .I jump from the top step of my Stoop and hit the ground running. I head down my block and leave her friendly confines as I turn onto Ave L, I can see Raymond Hart and his brother John walking a block ahead of me, I know we are all going to the same place. Other neighborhood kids join into our convoy as we pass by each block it grows larger and larger because they too are going to enjoy the fun that will be at our final destination.

We turn down 58th Street off of Ave L and there it is ....the Las Vegas to every Brooklyn kid whoever scraped a knee on the asphalt. It's The Park!!! It's The Park!!! The minute you enter the wrought iron gates that surrounded her a world of endless activities opened up to you and were yours and in which order you were to perform them was strictly up to you. It was ultimate freedom for a kid and choices were all yours. There was basketball courts with their unforgiving steel rims, there was baseball fields with mostly dirt and very little grass, but who cared,we were used to sliding into bases on the street!!There were the Handball courts which seemed to be the teenager's domain and was somewhat off limits to us youngsters. There were Monkey Bars made of steel connected bars that reached a good 15 feet at its top and if you were up there that made you King of the Monkey Bars (if Mothers today saw their children on these, they would go bananas). There were long thick wooden planks with to metal handholds on each end ...The See Saws, do you remember the person who was on the ground would threaten to jump off leaving to fall straight down? I used to like standing in the middle and balance them with my feet. There were the swings that made us believe we could almost touch the sky as we pumped our legs with all our might to reach the highest, without it starting to "buck" the chains that secured them. The Sand Box that to me always looked like a prison for little kids. There were the painted

Hopscotch boards. There were Kiddie Swings with that medal bar that came down as every Mother would always say "Now watch your fingers" as she slowly lowered it down to fasten their child into one. If you were thirsty there were the stone water fountains, that were never cold and you would have to almost press your face against the stone to get a drink because the pressure was so low. There was the stone mushroom like Chess Table that seemed to grow right from the concrete ground. The Park was a magical place that was our refuge from the streets and cars and our block and the watchful eyes of every Mother who spied on us as we played on the block. It gave us security to play the games of our youth and offered no interruptions because it was there for you to make your day everything you asked it to be.

By the way, can you guess who didn't make it home for dinner on time every Saturday? I will give you a hint ...His Mom calls him Mister.

Your Brooklyn

The Stoop

When I think back to the happiest times of my youth there is one place that is ever present. It was the place where I could view the world or what I considered it to be at that age. It was a place that I held many conversations with my parents and family.. It was a destination of safety when you needed to escape the troubles and dangers of everyday "Brooklyn Block" life. It was also a wonderful spot for us to play a sport and play records and conduct the simplistic acts of entertainment. It was the site of many meetings with other neighbors. It was where you hung out with your very best friends. It was a place that news and at times gossip was to be shared. It was where adults expressed their grown up opinions and children sang silly songs It was also a place that some of our life's milestones took place, I kissed my first girl there. In this world that we live in today people are always saying how much communication has broken down, I for one believe the disappearance of this place is partly responsible If you have not figured it out yet ...I am talking about .... "The Stoop". Do you miss that sacred spot as much as I do?

Your Brooklyn

The Tailor

It is the 70th Anniversary of the liberation of the Death Camp Auschwitz so in honor of an old friend I post this.

It has been 30 years since he has past R.I.P. Hymie...

I was 14 years old when I went to work at The Male Shop in Brooklyn on Ralph Ave. My job was to greet the customers who were there to pick up altered clothing and retrieve them from the tailor shop. I was called a "Take Out" along with 5 other guys who shared the same tittle. Beneath the store was a tailor shop where at least 25 tailors who performed their craft and trade .At lunchtime the other guys I worked with went out back to smoke pot. Now I am no angel but pot was not my thing so I sat in the tailor shop during lunch. I was just sitting there one day when this tailor asked me what I was doing. I told him I was just passing the time until my break was over. My answer seemed to anger him. He said in stern voice "You will not sit in my tailor shop doing nothing" He grab me by the arm and literally dragged me to his sewing machine and said "Sit down you are going to learn" The man's name was Hymie I began to get an education on being a Tailor. I spent my lunch hour every day at his side by his sewing machine as he patiently taught me a trade. He apologized for his anger when we first met and explained why he reacted the way he did. Hymie lost his family in the death camp of Auschwitz. His life was spared because a tailor had grabbed him and taught him his trade so he proved to be useful to the very murderers of his family. During the hours spent talking to him at "Our Sewing Machine" he taught me to cherish life and many other life lessons. He was simply the most amazing person because he held no hatred in his heart and that puzzled me. His philosophy was that he would neither hate nor seek revenge because neither could change what was the fate of his loved ones. He simply stated 'They are not allowed in my heart or mind." When Hymie passed on in 1985 I had a tree planted on a Kibbutz in Israel is his name ....I just said it was for...... "The Tailor"

Your Brooklyn

Brooklyn Cuisine at Its Best

I gather my football equipment into a U.S. Mailbag that last week I "borrowed "from the Post Office on Ave N and Flatbush. I ready my bike for the ride to Marine Park to play Hurricane Football. I slide my helmet onto the handle bar and place the bag on the bar and off I go. My Mom stops me at the end of the driveway and says "Don't forget your $1.50" How could I forget that? It was what I looked forward to after every game. The game has been played and win or lose our coach would give us a pep talk afterwards, he last words were always ..." Ok practice on Monday night, see you boys then". Now the race was on, myself and all my teammates make a mad dash for the cart with the yellow and blue umbrella. I make it there first...." Two dogs with mustard and kraut and an Orange Fanta"..I say .... "$1.50" is the reply. One of my fondest memories of Brooklyn was all the food and restaurants. To me there is no better place on the entire planet for Pizza. It is truly a melting pot for all culinary ethnicity Jewish, Chinese, Italian, Irish,German,Indian,Polish and so forth you name it Brooklyn's got it when it come to food. Yet there is one particular culinary feast that we can all agree on that is the best lunch in Brooklyn .... "The Dirty Water Dog"..... Where did you get yours from and what did you put on it?

Your Brooklyn

Nowhere On a Friday
Night in Brooklyn

It is a typical Friday night in Brooklyn. At my house we are just finishing dinner. Dad inquires as to who has homework and that it had better be done by Sunday Dinner. Tonight it is my chore to clear the table which I execute in lightning speed. I run up to my bedroom to begin my routine. I begin to select my outfit for this night. After 15 minutes of debating with myself I have made my final choice. I am going with my flowered Huck-A-Pao shirt, my Sergio Valente Jeans and of course my 3 inch blue corduroy platform shoes. Now the real fun begins I set up the ironing board and get out Moms Sunbeam steam iron. I fill the iron with tap water in the kitchen and begin my ritual. I get out my trusty can of Niagara spray starch and use enough on the crease of my Sergio's that only a nuclear attack could possibly cause them to wrinkle. My Huck-A-Poo is next and with surgical precision I place military pleats into the front and back of the shirt Into the bathroom I go to perform my 12 minute hair styling process that uses enough hairspray (Aquanet) to destroy the Ozone layer. Back to my bedroom where I ceremoniously don my gold "Rope Chain" necklace and bracelet. Now the final touch, I look at the top of my dresser and view the menu of colognes that will be my scent of choice for this Friday night...Pierre Cardin, Paco Rabanne, Canoe, Halston, Polo, Chaps...aha there it is I splash on my beloved Aramis and I am ready to go. I make a phone call to Peter who informs me that David Faillace, Larry Cassano, and Mike Marzigliano aand Evan Rosen will meet us there. As i am coming down the stairs I hear Peter beeping the horn of his Coupe De Ville which is to be our Chariot for this night. As I pass through the living room my Mom says "Where are you going?" I reply with the same answer we give our parents when they present that question... "Nowhere". She smiles and says to me "You spend 45 minutes getting ready to go "Nowhere?" I just smile back and kiss her on her forehead and in a sing song kinda way I say "Loove you Mom" and out the door I go.

You see, Friday Nights in Brooklyn were special to every teenager who lived there. You see any other nights during the week you could be just staying home doing nothing. You could have gone to a movie. You could have went to a friend's house just to hang out in the basement listening to the stereo and Eight Tracks. You could have just hang out with a friend and studied or did a science project together. You may have even gone to the mall to buy Fran Jolie's new record at Sam Goody's or maybe just walked around the mall or down the Ave and looked into the windows of the Jewelry Stores to see the 'Ankle Chains we would soon be buying and how much it would set us back. There were many things you could have done through the week but Friday Night in Brooklyn was something special

I hop into the Cadillac and we head out to our destination. Peter has chosen to wear his "Made in Brooklyn" Tee shirt and his best Sassoon's. He reaches down and pulls out a new cassette that Larry Cassano (The music guy in our crew) made for him, he pops in into the cassette player and Jackie Moore begins with "This Time Baby" and now the mood is set, we are ready, we are willing and we are able.

We are now officially "Crusin" The Ave. What was "Crusin"? one might ask well it was really just driving up and down the Ave but to explain what it meant to a kid in Brooklyn on a Friday Night well I can only say "Ya ain't from here so you don't git it."

We turn onto the Ave where we join in the metallic pageant formation with Grand Prix, Monte Carlos, Gran Torinos, Tornados, Eldorados, and all the other recently shined and polished cars with all the windows down and music blaring to the highest decibel possible. We roll down the Ave leaning back in our seats with an arm hanging outside the car. Staring, winking and whistling and doing everything possible and trying our hardest to get the attention of one of Gods most beautiful creations...The Brooklyn Princess as she walks with her best friends in all her splendor and hair...God they are gorgeous...one more prettier than the next.. Some smile some don't but that doesn't bother us because the night is just starting out .To me there was no place better to be on this planet than being... "Nowhere" on a Friday Night In Brooklyn"

Were you a Cruiser or a Princess?

Your Brooklyn

Cut Offs And A Tank Top

Cut Offs And A Tank Top

Cut Offs and a Tank Top. I put them on and look out my bedroom window to see if God is on board with my plan for this beautiful Brooklyn Summer day. I walk down the hall to my Moms linen cabinet and with jewel thief precision remove and item and sneak out the back door. In my Garage I mount my trust Green Schwinn 10 Speed and off I go. I approach E56th and Ave N and there I see Nick Blend Bobby Fitz and Joe Canning waiting as planned. We depart in single file and head out for Flatbush Ave. As we pass by the GreenLine Bus stop in front of Wetsons we can see alot of our friends who will soon be joining us at our planned destination. They wave to us and say "We will beat you guys there"......and they will.As we rode our two wheeled steel horses down Flatbush Ave we felt a sense of freedom as the wind was in our face...we were rebels with a cause. That cause being a chance to see our beautiful Brooklyn Princesses in Bikinis !!!! The bus now passes us by and we endure another round of heckling from our friends. We then arrive at the most dreaded leg of our journey. What to us seemed to be a mile of straight up peddling...The Marine Park Bridge!!! We look at each other and with Kamikaze Pilot determination we peddle as hard as we possibly can to reach the middle of this beast of a bridge.Each revolution of those sprockets brought on intense pain in our calves and thighs. Pushed to the point of sheer exhaustion we make it. Now like everything in life there is a reward for accomplished feats. Ours was that there would be no more peddling as we glided at frightening speed down the rest of the bridge and poor Fishermen would scramble in fear as we barrelled down towards them. It was surely like a scene right out of "The Little Rascals". Our destination is now in our sights.

We have now arrived at the Paradise of every Brooklyn Teenager.....
The Beach!!!!!!! My Beach was Riis Park Beach ....Bay 14 of course I step
to the sand and spot all our friends. Nick Blend produces a football and all
the guys rise up from their towels to join in a game of tackle in the sand.
We never really worried or kept score in those games. You see this game
was just to show off in front of all the Brooklyn Princesses. It seemed
that every once in a while the football would be "accidentally" thrown
dangerously close to the girl we most wanted to impress and we would
dive with reckless abandon to save her from being hit with it, in heroic
athleticism fashion. The reward for that magnificent feat was ... a smile...
and it was well worth it to us. The smell of coppertone mixing with the
salty sea air fills my nostrils as the sounds of The Hues Corporation's big
summer hit "Rock the Boat" is blaring from every transistor radio on 99x
(WXLO) drum in my ears. I find a spot on the sand and place My Moms
best bath towel down and I am set. As I look around to see all; the beautiful
L Park Girls Joyce Cataldo- Missy, Katie Mullady-Linda Carol Ronnie
Bruno and most of all the girl stole my heart Christine Destefano. The
hours of the day went by as we swam in the Atlantic Ocean. We chased
the girls along the sand, caught them (I know now they really wanted to
be caught) and dragged them into the Ocean. Then we would all make the
trip to the concession stand for a bite to eat. It was then I knew what it was
like to walk holding hands with the most beautiful girl on the beach, I felt
like the king of the world and I felt every guy on that beach were wishing
they were me. Thank You Christine, for letting me feel that way ..that day.
Hot Dogs and French Fries were on the menu and Coke or 7UP to quench
our thirst and then back to the sand and work on that elusive Golden Tan
that Coppertone promised we would all have The sun began to get lower
in the Brooklynsky which meant this magical day was nearing its end.
Everyone rolled up their towels and put their brushes and suntan lotions
in a bag and started heading back to the bus stop. We the rebels mounted
our trusty Schwinn Steeds and readied ourselves for the task riding back
home and of course doing battle with the dreaded Marine Park Bridge.
The beach was and always will be special to me because it was our getaway
from the streets. By the way Real Brooklyn Guys never wore a bathing
suit ...we wore...Cut Offs and TankTops

What Beach was yours?

Your Brooklyn

In Brooklyn All You Needed Was a Piece of Chalk, A Crayon, A Candle And a Bottlecap

A candle, a piece of chalk and a bottle cap was all we needed.

Growing up in Brooklyn was a magical experience that was afforded to all of us with the willingness to use our imagination.

It is another beautiful summer day and like every other summer day in Brooklyn my block is filled with kids because school is out and our time is our own. We would play all day long with sometimes a break for a quick lunch and if you didn't want to have lunch, well just make sure to be in the house for dinner at five. Nobody stayed in their house playing video games or watching Television.

This particular summer day for me begins as I finish my daily house chore and now I was free to "go out and play". I yell down the stairs 'Mom the hall and stairs are vacuumed can I go out now?",Mom comes upstairs for a quick inspection to make sure I used the long skinny attachment along the baseboards and around the banister pole .She smiles and nods her approval and I am free. I burst down the stairs and am almost to the door when I hear Mom say "' wait one minute Mister, who left their pajamas on their bed?"

Back up the stairs I run, I grab my pajamas roll them up in a ball and into my top drawer they go .*As* I open the front screen door Mom says "You didn't just roll them up in a ball and throw them in your drawer did you?" My head drops and I turn around to go back upstairs again when Mom just laughs and says "Go on... get out here and go play". It was her way of kidding with me and I loved her for that.

So to the launching pad (The Stoop) I go and as usual I jump from her fourth step and land on the ground running. I see Mike Miello on his stoop Joe Duval, Chris Smith Kenny Spinelli, Eddie Corloni are just leaning against Mrs. Timmons blue and white Studebaker with its huge whitewall tires talking to Mike over his fence.. The talk is what to do this day. Joe suggests that we go to the Park and play hard ball, so we all grab our mitts and head to the park. We get there and all the baseball diamonds are being used and there are other guys waiting for "Next". Back to the block we go .Chris says" lets play Running bases" which sounded great until we did a head count and realized we were about five kids short in our age group to play with. Kenny comes up with "Whiffle Ball" unfortunately our Whiffle Ball field was directly in front of Mrs. DeVito's house and she just happened to in her front yard tending to her prized Rose bushes. You see Mrs. DeVito was what we call a "Ball Keeper" so that was out because nobody was willing to put their Whiffle Ball in harm's way. So there we stood trying to figure out how to spend this day and with each passing minute we felt we were losing out on a good time. Then I don't exactly recall who said it out loud but we all looked at each other with that ...why didn't we think about this sooner look. We all scatter to our houses and hope to find what we need and be the first one back to the front of Mike's house. I am in a panic I found a bottle cap in the garbage can in the backyard, but I can't find a candle. So I grab the next best thing ...some old crayons. As I raced back I can see Eddie is already there making me second which wasn't bad. We all gather on the curb each with a bottle cap and a candle or crayon in my case. Mike lights his candle with a book of matches advertising Chesterfields cigarettes. He begins to fill his bottle cap by melting the wax into it. Everyone else follows suit except me. I wait for Mike to finish so I can borrow his candle to melt my crayon into my cap. We all lay our hot wax filled bottle caps on the curb and to cool down and harden. We all then look at Joe who was in charge of getting the chalk. He produces a thick light blue cylinder of chalk from his Dungarees pocket {notice I said Dungarees not Jeans) and we are about to draw our board .A eight foot by eight foot square is drawn right in the middle of East 55th Street, a box in each comer and two adjoined boxes between each of them with lucky number thirteen smack dab in the middle. Thirteen boxes in all and numbered one through thirteen. The object of the game was to slide your bottle cap into each box in numeric order and finish first without being killed by your opponents by hitting your cap with theirs three times .Yes people the game was Skelly!!!.....if you never heard of it ...then you are probably not from Brooklyn.

There were many other simple games that I played growing up on that block however this was one of my personal favorites. So that was our day as we all knelt on the hot asphalt a slid our caps into boxes jumped up and stood aside every time someone yelled "Car" and attacked each other's caps as if it was an Olympic event We played all day we all skipped lunch but made damn sure we were on time for dinner.

You see there was always something to do as we grew up on the streets of Brooklyn as kids. If you could not find something to do well then you just made up something to do, even if all you had was... a candle... a piece of chalk and a bottlecap!

Your Brooklyn

Once A Year My Block
Was A Concert

I wake up to another wondrous summer Saturday morning in beautiful Brooklyn. It is my thirteenth summer, and like all summers days it brings the promise of another day of sun drenched fun, friends and adventure. However there is something on this day that will provide just a little extra magic. It will combine the sometime separate parts of our lives that don't often get shared publicly. It is a day when we all got a chance to sneak a peek into the lives of others whom we call our friends and neighbors. My house and all of her 7 inhabitants are all up and we have our assigned tasks to insure the success of this yearly anticipated day. I look out the screen door that is the at the top of our stoop and my eyes witness a view that looks very strange.....no cars. The buzz is starting to fill the air and the sounds of each families preparations are can be heard and seen from house to house. It would seem that all the Dads would all be equipped with their green garden hoses with the twisting adjustable nozzle and like a well trained army they begin the task and the water sprays out to begin. Redwood picnic tables,mesh beach chairs, backyard lounge chairs, coolers, Bar-B-Ques begin to appear in front of all the houses on the recently "hosed down"asphalt street that would normally be the home for all the cars. In some cases even the beloved dinning room furniture would be summoned to outside duty.!!!!!! Then something happens that defines what this day is .....Brian Brian Leddy James Brennan and Anthony Eppolito who were all about 5 years old were riding their bicycles in the middle of the street!!!!!!!!... and neither of their Mothers were screaming.." Get back on that sidewalk Mister!!" I guess you all have now figured it out ....It's a BLOCK PARTY!!!!!!! On this day our family of grandparents aunts uncles and cousins were coming over as well as everyone else's on the block. It provided a chance for us to see each others families and meet them, because on any other day they would be in the confines of your living room or the seclusion of your backyard. No today you got to share and show them off to all right in front of your house. Sitting eating and talking right out there for everyone to see. And yet as weird as it looked ...it just seemed normal for just this one day a year. For me I just loved it because my favorite cousins who I would brag(my cousin William F. Gardner went to college and played basketball) about all the time were coming and I could introduce them to my friends, As night begins to fall the block takes on a whole different persona.The aroma of all the varieties of foods being prepared envelope the block andit is absolutely incredible .It seemed that every family sat down to eat at the same time and we all enjoyed our Dinner by the Curb" The loud sounds and voices seemed to become hushed as all my neighbors and us dined. Then just as dinner came to its conclusion and all your family members were all tended to it was time to visit with your neighbors. Every one got up from their tables and began to stroll up and down the block saying hello and tasting each other desserts .Mr DeVito always broke out his homemade wine for everyone to taste and enjoy. I remember so vividly the look of pride on his face as they all drank it. Fran Miello made the most awesome Macaroni Salad so I kinda wandered over her house to "say hello". Mrs Brennans specialty was a chicken and rice dish that was out of this world so of course I went over there to say hello to my buddy Phillip, not to mention the bonus of seeing his sister Linda who I had the hugest crush on. Mrs Nelson made her signature Swedish Meatballs and Mrs Corloni well she just made anything and it was to die for. Darkness now has taken over the block and 5long haired teenagers make their way through the crowds of people filling the middle of the street and proceed to set up their musical instruments. The band has arrived and it is no ordinary band .... It is Driftwood led by Louis LaRubio..was Larry Corvaiss,Jim Agnello Guy Speranza and Jim Powderly the hottest band in the neighborhood!!! The music they played through the night was cool and kept us all entertained as the block filled with people from other blocks who were all welcomed as they wanted to hear the band and dance in the streets with e rest of us. I guess my best memory was watching my Mom and Dad and all the other parents on my block dancing to "Brown Sugar", that what made it great at a Block Party you could do whatever made you happy. It is now about 2A.M. and the Block Party is over most houses are cleaned up and swept the tables are gone from the street and are being replaced with the cars that usually occupied its spot. The grills and coolers have all been put back in the backyards, it was a great day for all and just as I am ready to go to bed I look in the alleyway and there asleep on his Big Wheel is my my little brother Brian, a perfect ending of a perfect Brooklyn Day I miss those days and wonder if their disappearance has deprived us all of the closeness once shared by families and neighbors?

Your Brooklyn

Everyone in Brooklyn Had One ...And It Was Great.

Growing up in Brooklyn we often took things for granted, because we never thought enough about it to think that one day it would be gone.

Throughout my life growing up in my beautiful hometown that I called paradise there was always one thing that all generations and every walk of life that called Brooklyn home had in common. I will not drag it out this time ...I will just come right out and say it. It was shared amongst my Mom who used to religiously listen to Bob Grant every morning as she prepared the lunch boxes for my brothers and sisters and myself to keep up with the worlds politics which kept her in touch so that she could discuss the news with my Dad when he returned from work at the FDNY, to Mr. Rasmussen (He was the very first man on my block to leave his front door and head down to the bus stop for the B-41 to take him to the junction and begin his subway excursion to Manhattan) who waited for 1010 News to tell him that the subways were running on time. Then there was Mr. Roger Brennan who tuned in to find out if he would be wearing his signature cap (We Irish called it a Tern) if the weather report called for windy or cold temperatures that would call for covering his head. Of course there was always a time during the winter when the snow began to fall and to our delight it began to accumulate so every kid in Brooklyn sat and stared at it in the hope that their schools name would be mentioned withe word "Closed" in the same sentence. Michael Nelson who lived on my block would tune in to find out how his beloved (Even though they left Brooklyn) Los Angeles Dodgers were doing while everyone else on my block was much more interested in the The Amazin Mets or the all-powerful and seemingly unbeatable Yankees were doing.

There were those who just needed to be amused by the comedic stylings and antics of a guy named Imus as he pushed the envelope with his outrageous insights and borderline profanity. There some of us who as we rolled our beach towels into the very tightest cylinder we probably could and packed our Ban De Soleil for that deep Tropical Tan....and hoped to hear that it was going to be a great beach day with tanning index above 80.Then there was The WMCA Good Guys to inform us in each of their shifts as to which songs were the most popular on our listening air waves. There was Cousin Brucie (who was preceded by a legend we all called "The Wolfman") entertaining us with his banter and small business hawking. Nobody that I knew would ever ...ever miss Casey Kasem's weekly top ten and heartfelt dedications to starstruck lovers or our boys serving in the military across the seas. Later on Mr Joe Causi on WXLO led us all in the Disco scene and which were the hottest clubs to spend our nights at as we Hustled and danced the nights away in our favorite Discos.

There was Allison Steele (The Nightbird) who was our guide into the world of hard Rock-N Roll with her sultry voice and mesmerizing tone. Frankie Crocker who was the King of WBLS would signal every person in the realm of his voice at 7Pm ...Here I Go... Here I Go... Here I Go... John Montone with his unique voice on 1010 News was a staple in everyone listening in if indeed you were driving through our beloved Borough and it would always seem the BQE was jammed, the Gowanus expressway was bumper to bumper and of course...we all knew that the Mill Basin drawbridge was up and the Belt Parkway was backed up till Knapp Street ...right? By the way was there ever a time when someone said .... "Opposite side of the road parking was NOT in effect?"

Please let me also say one more thing... If you have never been within earshot of hearing "Saturday Morning with Sinatra" then you have no right to be reading this!!!

I know I said I was not going to drag this out....so freakin sue me! I did. Sorry about that.....The Radio ...Yes The Radio.

I am as guilty as anyone else today in the demise of what was once our lifeblood and sole informational source barring Television because I use my I-Phone and Computer today to relay all the information that I have previously stated. But God how I miss and will always remember hearing the click of that dial as I turned on that Radio and let the magic of all it had to offer fill my ears.

Don't it always seem to go that you don't know what you've got till it's gone?

Your Brooklyn

Jerry Lewis in the T.V. Guide meant Summer Was Over

The summers that I spent in Brooklyn growing up were some of the most wonderful days of my life. From that very first moment on that day in June, I raced home from school and took off my uniform, to me was when it started. The summer belonged to us and us to its carefree magical events. The days were longer and gave way to more time for our cherished summer activities.

The mornings with its early shadows and cooler temperatures made it prime time for a game of Stickball, Running Bases, or Whiffle Ball on the block. Hardball was played only in the Park to insure our parents having not to pay for broken windows and windshields. Basketball was also a Park activity because it was the only place that had hoops. The older kids ruled the Handball Courts of Ave "L' Park and John Zaccarias was its King, kinda the same way Michael Brennan ruled Baseball fields and Peter Bussola dominated in Basketball with their amazing athleticism

When twelve noon rolled around it was time for lunch and so everyone would scatter back to their homes for a quick Peanut Butter or Fluffemutter and Jelly sandwich and a glass of milk. I don't recall ever even chewing because I wanted to just get back out to the street as fast as humanly possible. I finish and into the sink goes that purple metal cup (it came in others colors but the purple one was mine). I am almost out the back door when My Mom says" Don't you leave a mess on my kitchen table." I catch the back screen door before it closes behind me and answer (in a sing song kinda way) "I knoooow Mom." I crumbled up the napkin along with the paper plate and chuck it in the square Tupperware garbage container with its triangular swing top and I am free to join my friends .The sun is hot now and it's time to turn our block into an amusement park ...yep you got it ....turn on the ...Johnny Pumps!!!

We spend the afternoon running through the spraying water as it soaked us all and cooled us down

Dinner time arrives and back in the house we all go. Only to be back out in a 1/2 hour to play in the remaining sunlight. All kinds of games are played 'til the sun goes down only to be interrupted by the always welcomed Ice Cream Truck.

This is pretty much what takes place on a daily basis throughout the glorious Brooklyn summer days which seem to us as if they will never end.

But then one morning you open up the T.V. Guide and your eyes gaze upon the sight that breaks your heart... a picture of Jerry Lewis and his advertisement for his Telethon ....this can only mean one thing.....Labor Day is here and summer is over. I am sure your summers were similar to this depiction of mine with some changes.

Let me ask you...What signs did you have to tell you summer was ending?

Your Brooklyn

Everett Scott A Brooklyn Tragedy

I have always referred to my beloved Brooklyn as if it's magic was a shield from all the bad things in life that confronted us but the inevitable truth is this...that was never the case ...the real case was that no matter where you are born and who you are, there is one thing that none of us can escape. That one thing is death.

As a great a place that Brooklyn was and is today, it was never immune to the passing of the people we loved and cherished. Even if they were taken unjustly and before their time. I am compelled to relate this story.

This will not be a feel good story like the ones I have relayed before, So if you are looking for a happy ending and a morale victory in the words you are about to read...then stop right now .This is an account of the murder of my best friend on the streets of my beloved Brooklyn.

I had long ago made myself a promise that if I ever came upon the chance to express my outrage and perception pertaining to the events that took my friend from me, I would not hesitate to tell his story. So if you are willing to continue, then I am honored that you do and it is my wish you understand my need I have to tell you about him when you have finished his story I hope you will understand.

His Mother called him Everett, yet as I remember she was the only person on this planet who called him that, which was his name. His Dad called him" Bobbie" and because he did everyone else who lived on East 55TH Street and anyone who was as fortunate as me to know him referred to him as such. The only exclusion I can think of were the Nuns of Mary Queen of Heaven, because after all they could call you anything they pleased and we would answer to whatever it was they called you. To everyone else on this planet he was... Boobie.

Boobie was only 3 years older than me but that was a lot growing up on my block where there were at least 10 kids of the same age ranging from 8to 18 and the gap seemed huge. However with Boobie age was never a factor to him he merely sought out anyone to have fun with...age, not an issue to him .Because our block was usually divided into age groups it was not the norm to see 16 year olds and 13year olds hanging together or playing together...it was just the way it was. Boobie however never adhered to those unwritten laws and included anyone who wished to participate in any activities he was involved in. I loved him for that and never forgot how great he made me feel when he invited me to play in his backyard. I tried to emulate him later on in the following years by treating the younger kids on my block the way he treated me. I think Chris Brown and James Brennan and my little brother Brian Leddy might now understand a little more now as to why I always tried to do the same for them.

Boobie was tall for his age maybe 6 ft. in his 16th summer and because of his height he was drawn to play basketball. His Dad knew it and built a basketball court in his undersized backyard with its Franklin backboard and orange steel rim and white netted hoop secured to the tin garage by 2x4s and molly bolts. The entire playing surface was maybe 15'x20' but to me it was like playing in Madison Square Garden alongside Walt, Willis, Dave, and Bill. We played endless hours with him in his makeshift court in his backyard and at times I knew he held back just to let us younger kids feel good about ourselves. Boobie was deadly from anywhere on that court and when he missed a shot... well let's just say it was because he never intended to make it, that's just the type of guy he was ....cool.

Growing up is sometimes the cruelest thing to happen to young boys, because they are forced to leave the nonchalant carefree days of our youth behind us .You see Boobie got older so much in just one year...the year he turned 18. He left the security of just being a kid and was testing the turbulent waters of manhood. The games in his backyard were now few and far between, his interest were now on the beautiful girls on our block (Betsy McNamara and Linda Brennan in particular). His thoughts were that of his future and the college he would attend to receive his further education I knew he was never going to hang around with us young guys forever but it really hurt to lose him to the dreaded adult stage.

Boobie was being looked at by colleges for his basketball skills and the whole block was abuzz with the offers that were being sent to his home every day, it was if he was the son of every parent on 55th Street because we all joined in the celebration of his success and going to college ...well you see that was something most parents on our block could only dream for their children.

Well I guess the oblivious next step getting ready to decide on a college was in front of him and that summer belonged to him. To his credit he never bought into his recruited celebrity but merely went about his life as usual. We still played three on three in his backyard and he still intentionally threw up a brick when he thought we needed a boost.

His decision was made in his mind and one night when I believe he sure of his next endeavor he went out with a bunch of neighborhood friends to celebrate his bright impending future at a local bar, Cavanaugh's on Ave N and Ralph Ave) and the celebration lasted to the early morning hours. Boobie left the bar with a buddy that early morning and while passing an early morning opening luncheonette, the alarm was ringing because the person opening that morning was new and did not know how to turn off the alarm .A Special Investigator for the District Attorney's Office was driving by and stopped, got out of his car and not knowing what was going on and didn't bother to ask. He saw Boobie and his pal standing outside the front door of the luncheonette trying to help the guy turn off the alarm .Without so much as a warning shot, and believing he was about to be a hero by thwarting a robbery he emerged from his car firing his revolver and Boobie no longer was alive. That bastard never thought about the kid who could hit a jumper from anywhere on the court...that bastard never thought about the kid who was about to start an amazing life....that bastard never thought about the kid who just kissed Betsy McNamara- goodnight...that bastard never thought about my best friend...... he just fired his gun

This was my very first experience with death and heartbreak, and I can tell you I still feel that pain...even as I am writing these words my eyes are blurred with tears. He was my friend ...he was my neighbor.....he was Everett Scott....he was Boobie.

He was everything I loved about Brooklyn ...he was my friend...and yet he was the only reason I ever, ever hated Brooklyn for what she let happen to him that night.

Brooklyn was to me and will always be a place that will always make me smile......but make no mistake Brooklyn can break your heart....and yet ...isn't that what life is all about? You take the good with the bad .... and that my friends....Is what Brooklyn is all about...Boobie was good...... his life stolen was bad....and Brooklyn was watching.

Your Brooklyn

The Diner ...Where All Brooklyn Nights Ended

Friday nights in Brooklyn were always waited for with great anticipation. It was the night that you were going out with either your friends or that special someone in your young life. You saved your money through the week just so you could make sure you had enough for the nights planned festivities. You were even willing to skip a few lunches throughout the week in order secure those plans.

Friday night is finally here so let the night begin. The options are endless, you may be meeting a group of your friends just to hang out at someone's house for a little party. It may have been that you were going to your local Bar to have a couple of drinks and hang out and play some pool and listen to the Jukebox at 7 plays for a a dollar.(Drinking age back then was 18) and if you are true to yourselves,you will admit that you were sneaking in at 16-17. Going to the movies with your girlfriend or boyfriend was always a great Friday night date. It was to me always cool to get there early enough to secure a seat in the very back row because it was nice and dark and there was no one behind you to watch you "making out"

Concerts of our favorite musical artists ranging from The Grateful Dead to The Rolling Stones to Marvin Gaye to Barry White and Barry Manilow were a mere train ride in to "The City", (which to me means Manhattan) at the Beacon Theater or Madison Square Garden .I remember always coming home with a Tee-Shirt.

I loved going to the many Discos in Brooklyn and get all dressed in our polyester suits and platform shoes and dance the night away looking at all those beautiful Brooklyn Princesses as they dazzled us with their enticing dance moves and sometimes the look of interest in dancing with us! "The City" had some great Discos as well but I preferred the ones right here in Brooklyn.

You may have just cruised around your neighborhood in your car with either your girlfriend tucked in right next to you under your right arm as you steered with your left(cuisine style). Or it may have been a car packed with your friends just taking in the night and stopping once in a while to "hang" on a corner now and then

No matter what you did, no matter where you did it, no matter who you were with, no matter what time it was. One thing was always a constant ending to whatever it was you did. Without fail as each one of my previous choices offered as your Friday Night experience, the night could not possibly be complete until you made the last stop before going home to call it a night.

Like nomads in the night's dessert we all flocked to that late night Oasis we know as The Diner!!!!!Yes guys the wonderful always there for you 24 hours a day Diner! We would sit there and relive the nights highlights as we enjoyed our Cheeseburger Deluxe chucked a couple of coins into the on the table Jukebox and happily let another Brooklyn Friday Night come to a close.

The Diner was home to so many of my Brooklyn memories and a place I always find in my thoughts when I think about my cherished friends of my youth. I can close my eyes and see each and every one of them and what they ordered as if it were just yesterday...God I loved that place!!! My Diner was The Kings Plaza and Arch Diner.

Which Diner did you call home?

Your Brooklyn

The Scent of Brooklyn

Here I am living in Long Island, it has been many years since I left my beloved Brooklyn. Every now and then I find myself missing her a little more than usual. It is then there is always something that will trigger a memory and I find myself in my mind right back on East 55TH Street in the midst of my magical childhood.

I have just completed my "Honey Do" list and the day is now my own... we'll see. The weekly ritual of manicuring the front lawn have been conquered and into the shed goes the mower. God I do love the smell of fresh cut grass.

To me there are certain smells that sometime can bring you back in time to very familiar places. Sometimes I can just close my eyes and be transported back to Brooklyn by remembering the smells and scents that flavored my youth.

On any given Sunday I could pass any house on my block and be intoxicated by the aromas that were escaping from the kitchens as the Moms performed their culinary magic for their families. Mrs. Corloni's sauce, Mrs. Kuzinskis Kilbassa, Mrs. Roththsteins Kreplach and all the other staple dishes that were a constant every Sunday.

I recall the smell of coffee filling my block every morning. I remember walking down the alleyways and taking in the scent of clothes being spun in a dryer in someone's basement as the silver vent released it in to the air. I remember my Mom hanging the laundry on the clothesline in our backyard and how wonderful it was to walk through the hanging bedsheets and smell that clean fresh detergent.

I remember the smell of leaded gasoline as the service man at the Sinclair Gas station pumped it into my Dads station wagon, then also the smell of the windshield washing fluid as it was sprayed onto the hot glass.

I remember the smell that would be fresh paint as Mr. Mueller prepared to paint the living room as he stirred it with what to me looked like a wooden ruler I used in school on his front stoop. I remember the scent of Windex could always be noticed as all the Moms on my block would be spraying and cleaning the "Storm Door" windows I remember the smell of Turtle Wax as Mr. Tolan shines his Pontiac to a high gloss finish. The smell that was on your hand after rubbing a brand new "Spauldeen" I remember the smell of Mrs. Ritters rosebush right after she pruned it. I remember the smell of motor oil as the Bracken brothers would jack up their cars right on the street and change their oil for the Hot Rods they drove.

I remember the smell of my test paper after it was freshly printed from the mimeograph machine in the office of Mary Queen of Heaven as it was put on the desktop in front of me I remember the smell of fresh tar on the base of the telephone poles on my block, you know the ones with the steel spikes that were there on each side so the "Bell" telephone repairmen could climb up those poles.

I remember the aroma of Mr. Rasmussen's cigar as he sat on his stoop listening to the voice of Phil Rizzuto on his transistor radio yelling "Holy Cow" as Bobby Murcer just made a helluva catch in center field at Yankee Stadium.

I remember the smell of the B-41bus as it pulled away from the bus stop and released its exhaust fumes with a swooshing sound.

I remember the smell of machine oil as the Grinding Man would be sharpening Mr. Petrolongos hedge trimmers in the back of his green truck as the Moms on my block stood in line with scissors and kitchen knives, it was also pretty cool watching the sparks fly from the stone hitting the metal.

I remember the smell of the generator of the Mister Softee Truck as I stood on line waiting for my "Twist" with rainbow sprinkles.

I remember walking past the local-luncheonette and the aroma of fresh bread and the bacon and eggs sizzling on the grill. I remember all different stores and the unique smells that would make me know where I was like ...the Pharmacy always bad that anti-septic clean smell the Dry Cleaners held that chemical clean smell the butcher shop with that magnificent scent of sawdust that when you stood in every time you were in there, you just could not help yourself but to push it into little piles with your feet and of course the smell that you experienced as you turned down the aisle in the A&P and it's 8 O'clock Coffee grinding machine.

However with all this said the one smell that really says Brooklyn to me is ...the sweet aroma of the burning hot July Asphalt as the steam rises it from it after a torrential downpour of rain. I would like to think Heaven will smell something like that.

Want to share your smells?

Your Brooklyn

Brooklyn She Is At Her Most Beautiful When She Is Sleeping

Itis not quite four o'clock on in the morning on my eleventh Brooklyn summer. My Dad enters the bedroom that I share with my brother Michael. He wakes us and we quit as Church mice dress and descend our stairs trying not to step on that that creaky step so as not to wake Mom, my sisters and baby Brian. Dad opens the fridge and removes a square plaid vinyl bag with the sandwiches and preparations made by Mom the night before. We exit through the front door in complete silence as though we were cat burglars. My block is deserted and quit as only the streetlights are awake with us as they act as sentinels keeping the block safe.

The three of us find Dads Plymouth custom suburban station wagon parked in front of the Tolans house. We hop in the car Dad navigates the car towards Flatbush Ave and our journey is under way. As we drive I can sense that there is an almost eerie silence that exists. Michael Dad and myself know where we are going and there is no talking as we are somewhat still half asleep For Brooklyn and most of her inhabitants are still in their slumber as only the night people like ourselves this morning get to gaze upon her utter beauty as she sleeps. The absence of her people hustling and bustling along her streets and the symphony of the cars and voices gives her a calm and serene feeling only to be experienced in the wee hours of the night.

A New York Daily News truck slows down in front of the news stand just enough to let the man in the back of the truck throw his newspaper bundles and make them land directly in front of it. A little further down the Ave a green Savinos private sanitation truck is stopped in front of Nana

Daleys removing the contents of its dumpster. A bakery truck is delivering the morning's bread and rolls to the local luncheonettes and restaurants. The cabbies pass by with an occasional late night inhabitant most likely the last customer to have closed a nearby bar or tavern .The B-41 bus is a strange sight to be seen as she rolls down the Ave with not a soul on her aside from her driver who is making his last run of the night before heading home to his sleeping family. The squad car with her night patrolmen of the 63rd precinct slowly creep along the Ave to make sure that no harm will come to us and the businesses of our beloved Brooklyn...not on their watch. They are our guardians of the night and keepers of our laws. The street signal lights continue to change colors as if they don't even care that there are no cars or people to heed their illuminated warnings and directions, A beam of light from each streetlight attaches itself to our car and hands us off to the next streetlight as if to guide us down the Ave. I swear to God the Moon was following us.

Dad has us going onto The Belt Parkway as we pass by Nicks Lobster Floyd Bennett store and The Marine Park golf course all with no signs of movement or life as we exit Flatbush Ave. The Belt in one of the only times in my life was actually empty and it gives us a feeling that we are the only people left on Earth. Our ride on the Belt is short because Knapp St exit is here and we take it and find our way to Emmons Ave .We near our destination as we can see and smell salt the water of the ocean and a stretch of bright lights that stand out above the decks attached to the masts of these huge fishing boats and announces that this place is awake and waiting for us. Sheepshead Bay ...the nautical crown jewel of Brooklyn!!!

The Captains of the ships sit on a chair at the beginning of the slip which docks their ship of trade announcing their itinerary and which fish is to be their quarry, the aroma of the mates preparing the bait fills the air (for better or worse). Their voices pierced the quit slumber of the night as it was about to give way to yet another glorious Brooklyn summer morning.

We leave the dock aboard the majestic Helen V heading to the ocean .As I look back over the bow of this ship, I can begin to see lights appearing in the houses and cars beginning to occupy the streets, I can see Brooklyn waking up and alive and showing life as most of us view her on a daily basis, as the commotion of her everyday life begins to take shape. This is where she is at her best, when the people like you and me and all of our fellow Brooklynites live our lives and routines and fill her streets, and drive our cars, and work in our shops,and take our kids to school and sweep our sidewalks and do our shopping and talk to our neighbors .Yes her best is when all these things I mention are happening all at once and she hums with the life blood we infuse in her with our everyday lives, but I gotta tell ya...... she is to me at her most beautiful when she sleeps. Good Morning Brooklyn ...I hope you slept well

Your Brooklyn

Happy New Year Brooklyn Style

The gifts have all been opened and the hugs and kisses of gratitude have all landed on the proper cheeks of family members and friends. You take inventory of your proceeds and in your mind you have already put those gifts into play.

Itis my seventeenth year celebrating Christmas in my beloved Brooklyn and just as the past sixteen before… it was wonderful and filled with glorious memories. However that is not where the Holiday Season ended in Brooklyn… well at least the way I remembered it.

It was my senior year in High School and Christmas break was to last till January 3rd. Which meant that this was a very special time for a young boy and girl in Brooklyn. You see as strict as our parents were, they knew that this was the year that we chose to be the year to exercise the limits of our freedoms and test the waters of adulthood.

My Mom and Dad were getting dressed to go "down the block" to one of the neighbors' homes to celebrate,It seemed that on my block (East 55th Street) every year the celebration would at a different home every year and it went that way, kinda like a cycle and this year it was at the Baxters house. They knew what my plans were and either chose to not make a big deal of them or just let me enjoy them and make me feel the moment.

I am in my room blowing my hair and when it it perfectly coiffed I apply enough Aquanet Hair Spray to make sure that even if I get caught in a Hurricane this night …my hair will not move(Anyone who still knows me today will understand what I mean and how important my hair is to me). Now the task of choosing just the perfect three piece polyester suit to wear is my next dilemma. It just has to be the right suit because I know everyone who I will see tonight will be wearing their very best and I must be equal to the task. I select my tan three piece and get out my dark brown Oleg Cassini silk shirt. I with my left hand use my forefinger and my thumb to open the clasp of my 14kgold rope chain with the diamond studded lightning bolt and with my right hand slip the loop inside the open clasp and release it to the locked position it falls around my neck and is a sign to all that I am cool., I step into my tan corduroy platform shoes and am ready... well almost ready. I gaze upon my dresser top and scan to see what cologne will be the one best compliment the night...... it was down to two ...Aramis or Paco Rabanne. The girl I was taking out that night loved Aramis ...guess what I chose.

In every seventeen year old girls bedroom from Canarsie to Bay Ridge who was going out that evening with their boyfriends, or just with the girls the preparations were three fold more intense than what I considered to be my preparations that evening .The nails, the toe nails, the pantyhose or stockings, the hair that was sure to make Farrah Fawcett jealous, the perfect pants, top or dress the scent of Babe, Shalimar. Jontue or Halston perfume hung in the air and most of all ...the most magnificent pair of Candies wooden heeled spiked heels to match the ensemble and in my case my girlfriend adorned a full length Sheepskin Coat that made her look like the Queen of Brooklyn ...and to me she was .

For this unprecedented night that will allow me and my girl to come back home after 3AM without reprisal from our parents. !!!!!!This night to me and others was an almost coming of age for those of us who were lucky enough to call Brooklyn our home. On this night I am taking my girl out for a night on the town.

We meet our friends at 9pm at a bar in Mill Basin called "After Midnight" and we (I am well aware that we are seventeen, but drinking age was eighteen at the time so sue me)

Cataldo-Serpico Christine Destefano-Weiss Linda Puma Nick Blend Bobby Fitzpatrick Michael Kuzinski Greg lpVerde Debbie Schmidt Susan Susan Schmidt- Katie Mulady-Fahey. Missy Kuzinski John Zacharias, John Hart Joe Canning Jane Atwood Maria Mangano Jackie Cuccarullo Karen Ferrone The Scalfanis The Brajas .The Storrz and all other friends I fail to mention enjoy a couple of cocktails and then leave for our final destination We are going to a "Club" called The Chateau Blue .on Foster Ave and 49th Street because our friend Frank Serpico's Dad owns the joint and he said it was ok for us to go, and if Franks Dad said it was OK and safe ...well you just knew it was (if you get what I mean) So in case you have not guessed it yet ....it is New Year's Eve in Brooklyn! !!!!!!!

We arrive at Chateau Bleau and the DJ is playing the music loud (Disco) and the place was ours. Every time the door opened up and a new couple walked in it was as if they were another contestant in a contest for best dressed (I ain't bragging but I thought me and my girl took first place) .The club was filled with the most beautiful creatures God himself ever created,,,The Brooklyn Princesses !!!!!!We "Hustled" and slow danced and made out on the dance floor as we held each other close and it seemed as if the night would last forever and it almost did... The magical moment swept over us as the music stopped and a strange silence filled the joint as we all turned our attention to a 19" television that sat behind the bar...Dick Clark counted down to 12:00 and as if we had practiced for this moment all our lives ....we screamed and jumped up and down like lunatics making as much noise as possible. Then I took my girl in my arms and realized how happy it felt to kiss someone you loved to start a New Year just like my Mom and Dad did!!! We danced .we sang and we drank Champagne all night long till the hands on the clock announced that the evening was to be no more and that morning was not too far off. We all felt so cool that night because we drank from the forbidden glass of growing up.........and we liked it. Saying goodnight to every one of my friends that night as we left the club seemed somewhat strange. The kids that I met at "After Midnight" were not the same people I said goodnight to as we left "Chateau Bleau" They all seemed to be different ...or just maybe older.

Car service dropped me and my girl at her home on 59th Street and Ave L. it was almost 4:30 in the morning. I kissed her goodnight at her door and began to walk back home to 55th Street. As I walked down Ave L at that hour of the morning with just the street lights as my company I felt as if being out this late alone gave a message to me ...It was not just a "New Year" this year........ It was an introduction to a new life.

I am proud to say that from that year forward my New Years have been progressively better and I have enjoyed each and every one of them....Yet I will always remember that night in Brooklyn when that New Year's Eve gave way to a new life (Growing Up).

Happy New Year Everybody!!!

Your Brooklyn

I Said Goodbye To Brooklyn But Never Stopped Loving Her

How does one say Good Bye to Brooklyn?

There was only one thing on this planet that could ever have dragged me out of Brooklyn and make me say goodbye to her.

This is how my Brooklyn story ended.... for now....some of you might say ....Thank God.... and I hope some of you will enjoy it.

I have attempted to recreate my recollections and my fondest memories of my youth(whether or not you have read my past writings) and growing up in the most magical place on earth outside of fantasy and downright wishful thinking, for others and that is ....Brooklyn .... It all started there and it is my hope it will all end for me there sometime in the distant future

.... This has been an accurate diary of all my life growing up in Brooklyn, if you have read my past posts.

I have tried with my best verbiage to bring you all back to that place where the magic just took control of us and to our lives it just took in a whirlwind and delivered us to a place wherever we landed and in all its splendor, continued to drive us all to where we all are today and who we are at this moment. I have with all my heart and fondest truths and sincere memories attempted to bring you all back to a place where it all began and to a life that sometimes seems to be another lifetime ago that I deem to be my own story, because this was the life and times and adventures that we all can call our beautiful home......Brooklyn.....She afforded me the setting for my story, yet I share with each and every one of you a familiar recollection, and I feel you will enjoy the memories. In the hope that you too shared the same black and white Polaroid pictures and 8 millimeter visions of yesteryear that I possess in my mind and will stay with you as much as a Polaroid picture that you all keep within an old year book or bottom drawer you call your memory box. Yes my friends I speak and write passionately of ...Brooklyn.

One just might in my way of thinking, ask why it is that I left, and that would be a valid question but it is my passionate belief that where we all came from, has played a major role in where we all are today, whether that be good or bad...you fill in your own story. You will soon know my reason if you read on

I speak with such reverence of this place that one might have pause to ask why I left? The answer is quite clear in my mind ...but I will leave it to you as to what the telltale reason is. I am in the nineteenth year of my life and just another Brooklyn kid searching for direction and meaning and his destination in life and that thing that is called the elusive "infinite wisdom" ... and just what this world holds for me, in other words I am as confused and oblivious as to what this life has in store for me and what part it asks me to play in this ongoing drama and perform as the days in front of me unfurl and presents its options to me and what my reactions should be..

It starts out to be like any other Thursday night... except Peter Bussola calls me and tells me that we are going to Lynbrook Long Island to a place called "Hot Skates" instead of our usual place. "The Roller Palace" in Sheepshead Bay where we called our "Roller Skating home". I along with Peter Bussola, Evan Rosen, David Faillace Larry Cassano Mike Marzigliano and Chrissy Zarzano(R.I.P.) Worked as "Skate Guards" and then all the friends we called our "Skating Friends" such as Lisa Ferranti-Sciortino, Gina Ferranti, Susan Barnartan, Deborah Sclafani Montano, Ann Marie Russo, Helen Proveromo, Annette, with Judy Massimillo spinning the vinyl and securing another musically great time and others .We are heading along the Belt Parkway to Sunrise Highway to a place called Lynbrook which might as well been in Asia, but it was the home of "Hot Skates"

I select from my closet a pair of white tight fitting "Chinos" and a Powder Blue short sleeved shirt with cuffs on the sleeve that I personally ironed in. I am ready to show Long Island just what guys from Brooklyn can do on skates. We park our cars and walk to the entrance and am quite surprised when we realize we actually have to pay to go into the rink (We were all Royalty and never paid to skate...in fact people in Brooklyn paid to see US skate) we paid the $7 bucks for the first time in our lives to skate ...and in we went. We laced up our own Chicago Skates (We never rented) I looked at Peter and we gave each other "The Look'....No words had to be spoken we were here for one thing and one thing only "Let's light this joint up" is the look we gave to each other." We skated at speeds that were normally reserved for the Roller Derby and performed jumps and moves as even the D.J. I know just how lame this sounds as I am writing it)) Now I don't know what Long Islanders did when they skated but what we threw out was ...no doubt...something they never seen before. Guys held their girlfriends a little bit closer that nigh...and for good reason. We took over the place and we knew (shit, we just spent $7 and we were gonna get our money's worth)

We spun, we did things on skates that people watching us never dreamed were possible we skipped, we "Sakowed" and in my case we "Cartwheeled" on skates. We knew we were Kings inn this joint(I realize just how pretentious that sounds but we were that freakin good) and everyone took notice of these Brooklyn Kids and their skills.

One particular Girl took notice of this one Brooklyn kid who did three consecutive Cartwheels on skates(My usual routine to attract girls) and found me after intermission. She asked if I would do a cartwheel for her and her friends. I had only to look into that girls eyes and knew if she had asked me to do a cartwheel over Snake River Canyon I would have done it without a parachute! She owned me and I was willing to be owned .Without having to go into detail, this girl was like no other girl I met before and believe me when I tell you she was no Brooklyn Princess but she was something more, she. She captured my heart that particular night and the life I so adamantly fought to hold onto was no longer mine. She was engaged to another the night we met,...three weeks later the engagement was off....she chose me and I gave up every girl I was dating at that time (although my Mom might tell you a different story) because ...she was the one....yes she was the one...she was the one who I fell in love with ....she was the one who I wanted to marry... she was the one who made think... there are other places ya know other than Brooklyn.... yes... she was the one to make me leave Brooklyn .

It was love....Let me repeat that ...it was love...It was the love of a young woman with incredible eyes who loved Steely Dan and The Eagles whom possessed all the qualities that I expected of the woman to fulfill my dreams. Yes it was love that made me be willing to change the Zip Code and The B-41 for the L.I.E, it was that 4'11" girl who made me exchange

Eisenhower Park from Prospect Park....it was a girl who made me go to the Riverhead Museum instead of the Coney Island Aquarium ...yes it was! Yes she was the one for whom I left Brooklyn for ...yes she was the one who I knew at the time would fulfill my destiny ....yes she was the one who seduced me to leave my one true love... Brooklyn.

She as it turned out to be was not "my true love" Yet she did give me one of the most wonderful gifts of my life....my son Nicholas and yet without her I would have never met my true love (and I would like to think, she would have not met hers). She also allowed me to find what we all look for and search out for our lives....my soulmate ....My Bride Robin...who has blessed me with two wonderful children and a life of happiness that should be afforded to every man who is lucky enough to walk on this planet if they are willing enough to recognize the gift of a wonderful woman when she grabs you in a phone booth and passionately kisses you unexpectedly, that is another story for another time.

So that is what made me leave Brooklyn, I traded one very special woman in my life for another...I left Brooklyn ....it was Love....The only thing that could drag me away from the seductive woman that is Brooklyn .....to me she will always be my first love...she will always be my home....she will always be the place that I will find the loving arms to comfort me when life shows its's most ugly and menacing side. She has never judged me nor did I ever give her cause to question me... I never left you... Brooklyn... and I will never call any other place home your warm arms and bountiful bosom is where I will forever find my safe haven and the one and only place that allowed me to become who I am today.... and for that I will be in your debt forever

So you see my fellow Brooklynites it was Love ...pure unadulterated Love.... It is what made me a Brooklynite from my birth to my first kiddie party to my first dance, to my buying an Ankle Chain to my first dance, to my first fishing trip and the site of Brooklyn from a fishing boat out of Sheepshead Bay at 4:30 am to my first block party, to my first snow storm, to my first game of "Skelly" to my first whiffle ball game, to my first "stickball" game to my first game of "Ring-0- Livio" to my first game of "Johnny on the Pony' my first game of "Freeze Tag" to 'Riding the B-41" To Prospect Park to Having your Birthday at Jahns(Kitchen Sink) n to Roll -N- Roasters to Brennan and Carrs to Juniors Cheesesteak to Di Frara s Pizza to Dubrows on Kings Highway to The Male Shop to Kings Plaza to The Leading Male on Kings Highway to Lesters on Ave

U to The kings Plaza, Floridian.,Seaview, to the Arch Diners and all the other diners not mentioned to Gimbels and Macys,Mays, Alexanders and A&S, Korvettes, Times Square Stores, and to Ideals on Flatbush Ave and to Money Savers and The wonderful bars of my youth ...Herbs, Club 52, Kavanaughs, Faheys, The Camelot Inn (which I named my business after) Floods on 37th St, Cafe Milieu (where I knew to never repeat what I heard) Scandals Freds Hideaway on Emmons Ave to The golden Dove on Third Ave to Wheelers on Sheepshead Bay Road where I worked to The Salty Dog To The American Legion on Ave N (You getting the feeling I went to a lot of bars) and of course The Gemini Lounge where I worked and learned that there was a dark side of life (they were people in a life that I will never understand ...A dark side of Brooklyn that few will understand and most will look upon in disgust... They were my friends and I make no apologies.... enough said).

To all the Discos and especially 2001 Odyssey where we drove our cars around the block from 2am till 6am trying to get ourselves in the movie "Saturday Night Fever' ...there was the Theaters ..The Mayfair.... The Kings Highway ...The Brook, The Marine...and others. If I get into the restaurants I could go on for days ....not to mention the Hot Dog Stands and Kosher Delis and Pizzerias. My God we were lucky!!!

I don't have to name all the places and things we use to do ...do I? Of course not because you lived it just as I did, My story and stories that I have written are NOT just my stories they are

... YOUR stories. What makes them so unique is that they are not just mine! You see the stories I write to which some people may think are just MY stories.... You know different... because you are from Brooklyn. All you have to do is just insert different names and dates and places ...and they are YOUR stories ...YOUR life in Brooklyn. Hell I just have been writing all the things you experienced... We are the same people.........Who lived the same life!!!!

Yes there are different places ....Yes there are different names ...but the culture was almost exactly the same.

So please don't believe for one moment that I ever left Brooklyn for no good reason... It was Love....Yes it was love... It was the love of another woman and she (My Bride Robin) and I know Brooklyn understands... why I have stayed away?

To me I don't know if I could ever recreate the magic that once was .... choose to visit often and enjoy how she has grown up with me. But if you are a True Brooklynite ....you know one thing.....You Never Forget Your First........Brooklyn was It is my intention to publish my writings and invite you all to be a part of this Book ...because you ARE a part of it. I am presently in negotiations with a couple of Publishing Houses and it seems I might need your permission to use your past replies to my posts in my book .I also would like to use some pictures that relate to my past posts if youse guys got any and you don't mind sharing, hey pass it down will ya Joi ...Also if you know somebody in the publishing game or you "got a guy or a hook" let me know...you know us Brooklynites are always looking for a better deal

Hey listen, I am real happy you all have read my posts .This is the last before the book. I would have never thought of writing it without your positive input and encouraging thoughts (hell I am just a guy from Da Neighborhood) and it is because of your responses Publishers are taking me seriously and for that... am eternally grateful.

By the way......If you read the first line in this post...I'll never say Good-Bye to Brooklyn... I'll just say... Catcha Latta!

Seriously I hope you enjoyed reading YOUR book.

Kevin J. Leddy

Your Brooklyn

On A Beautiful July Day

It was an incredibly hot summer afternoon. My nerves were on edge and I was sweating on the altar at church. Then as the doors in the back of the church opened ..my life changed. You appeared there and my eyes held the vision that was you. I know the church was packed but in my eyes it was just you and me. You moved down the aisle as if your feet never touched the ground and my heart was no longer mine. It might have been moments later when Pastor announced us man and wife ...but we were married before you stepped onto the alter, It did not need to be said to me by anyone. You have given this man a wonderful life and blessed me with our precious children. You have stood by me professionally, spiritually and emotionally. My love for you has never been stronger as that very day and I will continue to honor you for the rest of my life. I know that people sometimes snicker or laugh because I always refer to you as "My Bride" ..Robin and I don't care...because if they knew the feeling I had that day they would understand and I pity them and everyone else on this planet because you are mine and they will never know the wonder of what that means to me. Happy Anniversary to "My Bride".

Your Brooklyn

Robin

Friday night my bride Robin and I were invited to a nightclub for a friends birthday. Thank you Dawn and Scott Rogers.

It has been years since we have danced together except for an occasional wedding. We were having a ball and feeling younger than our years. After finishing a dance I went to the bar to get a drink for us. When I returned there was three guys in their late twenties standing around Robin. I stopped and paused for a moment and realize these guys were hitting on my wife! Years ago I would have handled this ..let's say differently and leave it at that. Only this time I just stood there and smiled. Robin was being graciousand polite as she spurned their advances. I then realized that these three guys were seeing the same thing I see when I look at her. I would like to thank those three guys for reminding me just what a beautiful girl I get to be with every night!!

Your Brooklyn

DOC

The anticipation was growing and I would be lying if I told you I wasn't nervous. It was November 6th 1985 and you chose this day to change my life. Your Mom announced to me that her water broke and the mad dash to the hospital began. I had been waiting for nine long months to meet you and it would appear that my wait was coming to an end. Your Mom was amazing and brave. I on the other hand found myself a little shaky to say the least.

You were just about to make your grand entrance into this world when your head and right shoulder were peeking out. At that moment the doctor said to me "Would you like to bring your child into the world?" I looked into your Moms eyes as she held a death grip on my hand and asked her if that would be alright with her. She in no uncertain terms let me know that I could do whatever I wanted as long as it would make you come out as soon as possible.. So there I was with one hand on your tiny head and the other gently gripping your right shoulder. The doctors told me to pull gently as your Mom pushed and right on cue after the third push,you slid right into my arms. I was beyond shocked as I held you for the very first time. I shouted "Doc...Doc...what do I do now?". "Hold your baby to your body for warmth" was the answer. As I held you as close to my chest I could feel your little hands clutching my shirt and wished you would never let go....forever. That as you know is the reason I have called you Doc all your life, you see it was the very first words you ever heard and when I call you Doc I always remember that moment.

Nicholas Adam "Doc" Leddy It has been one fantastic ride since that day and I have enjoyed each and every moment sharing it with you from spending a whole weekend in a tub filled with Oatmeal Bath when you had the Chicken Pox to chasing down the person who hit your car that night when you were twenty-eight .....It wasn't him..

You continue to warm me by you sharing your life with me as I shared my warmth with you on that November day not so long ago and for that I will always cherish and be thankful .I Love you Doc

Your Brooklyn

Garrett

Just about 13 years ago I was running behind a bicycle with my hand on the seat. A terrified little boy was screaming "Daddy don't let go.... please Daddy don't let go" I assured him I was right there and would not let him fall. I ran behind the bike until I could keep up no more. I watched that little boy conquer his fear and gain his independence all in in one fleeting moment. Today 13 years later that little boy will at 1PM Eastern Standard Time strap himself into the cockpit of a plane at Embry Riddle and will achieve in his plane what he achieved on his bicycle. I wish I could run behind the plane on the tarmac and hold onto the tail of the plane but I know this time he does not need me because he already has his independence and he no longer gives into fear. So to my son Garrett please know that although you may be flying solo today I am always your co-pilot at heart.

Garrett completed his solo flight with "flying colors" no pun intended. He scored a 100% Grade and his certification is complete. I say these words with immense pride and admiration for him. He called me when he landed and his voice sounded somewhat different. I don't know if it was excitement, relief or it was maybe that for the first time I heard him speak as a man. Something happened up there and I can see that it changed him in a positive way. I know that he is feeling great accomplishment .I guess he now feels the world is welcoming his dream with open arms. As I always told Garrett when he was growing up.... "The Skys the Limit to all your Dreams".....maybe I was wrong, he has shown me that there are no limits to his dreams. The Sky or otherwise. I love You Garrett

Your Brooklyn

Jacqueline, My Little Girl

Even with her very first steps, daddy's little girl walks away. It is inevitable and there is nothing you can do to prevent it. It begins with crayons and coloring books and then before he even realizes it, she graduates from elementary school to middle school and probably her most dramatic movement is into to puberty. Make-up, nail polish, and hair care products become familiar sights that dominate your bathroom. Soon enough she is a junior in high school, driving a car, going on dates with boys, and attending school dances and later Proms. Then comes the biggest step yet: moving away to a university or college. Despite the continuous change, this little girl's daddy can rely on a stable relationship with his daughter, knowing that she is never too far from his reach. Fathers and daughters share a special bond, unlike any other. She his treasure, and he her hero. I know that I trust her, I know she is responsible, I know she is all grown up now....what I don't know is how to keep my heart from aching as she waves goodbye to me as I drive off her campus. Jacqueline, I will just say the words I have whispered into your ear every night of your life as you put your head on your pillow to sleep............'Jacqueline you are the most beautiful little girl in the whole wide world...and your Mommy and Daddy love you very much"

Well here I am sitting in the auditorium waiting for the graduation ceremonies to commence for Jacqueline. I am reading the program and college choices of her class mates. Next to Jacqueline name is Mercy College. I recall the process that we as a family went through to get to her decision. Jacqueline was sought after by many schools who offered her full scholarship to attend because of her outstanding Cheerleading skills. They recruited her with unwavering vigor and made her choice even more difficult. Then about 6 months ago she sat down with my Bride Robin and myself and this is what she said. "Mom 'and Dad. I have given all. my offers strong consideration and I feel that Mercy is my choice because my mind and my heart tell me it is the place for me." I asked her why and she said" Cheerleading is a passion that I will always have in my heart but Mercy offers me the best opportunity to achieve my goals in Physical Therapy and that is where my future is" You see Mercy does not offer a Top Cheerleading program but it is one of the very best in the nation in Physical Therapy. Now she will be stepping on stage in about a hour from now and the State of New York will hand her a diploma and recognize her graduation. However to me she graduated the very night she told us of her decision to attend Mercy; because that diploma only says she completed her schooling but her decision told me she is all grown up and making adult decisions. I won't claim to love my daughter any more than any other parent loves theirs but I will say that I dare to say none are any prouder than I am at this moment. Jacqueline my world will always be brightest with you in it and it will never matter where you are on this planet .... I am there with you. You are my daughter and for that I will always love you........You are my friend and for that I thank God. Congratulations to .... "The most beautiful little girl in the whole wide world....and your Mommy and Daddy love you very much" I love you Jacqueline

Your Brooklyn

Dads

Dads are the biggest source of strength for a child. The innocent eyes of a child perceive father as the all-powerful, most knowledge, truly affectionate and the most important person in the family. For daughters, fathers are the first men they adore and fall in love with. While for sons their fathers are the strongest person they know and someone they aspire to emulate. Even for the grownups fathers are someone whom they look up to for the most experienced and honest advice that is always in the best of our interest. For this great figure in our life that we know as father - it becomes our utmost duty to pay our humblest tribute on the occasion of Father's Day.Children blessed with a loving father should consider themselves fortunate. For, they have someone to take care of their needs and interests. Someone to stop them when they are diverting to a wrong path and guide them on a road to success and virtue.. Fathers would never ever give a smallest of hint to let us know how hard they work to take care of our needs and fulfill even the most whimsical of demands... For all their adorable scolding and affectionate punishments we all owe a big thanks to our Dads.

We must make all efforts to celebrate Father's Day with our Dad.. The idea is to show our affection and tell Daddy how much he is loved and appreciated not just on Father's Day but every single day of our lives. So to all the Dads here in our little group and to their Dads and most of all all the Dads who are no longer with us Happy Fathers Day I would also include all the Single Moms who must be both Mom and Dad ...and on a personal note to my Dad Geno Leddy ....I Love You First!!!!!!!!!

Your Brooklyn

Hey Pop Pop you know what? We love you first
(L to R back row) Nick Leddy, Angelica Leddy, Michael Leddy,
Harley Rae Leddy Nicole Leddy, Gena Viviano, Theresa Leddy ,
(L to R sitting down) Maryann Leddy, Kevin Leddy, Geno Leddy
Michael Leddy Eileen Leddy.
Brooke Leddy Sean Leddy Connor Leddy
and Bridgid Leddy (on the floor)
The Brooklyn Leddys

Acknowledgments

The People Who Made Brooklyn the Magical Place For Me ....Thank You All

Michael you are the toughest guy I knew growing up, Thanks for looking out for me when we were kids without you there is no book, Thank you for being there

Eileen whenever I felt I was alone as we were growing up I knew I could always talk to you. You should know how much I relied on you Thank you for being there

Maryann I know that I teased you often while we were growing up, but let me tell you something. You have the kindest heart of any one on this planet. Thank you for being there

Brian you were "The Baby" However you are truly the best of us and it is my wish for my own sons to be half the man you are today. Thank you for being there

My Nana Catherine Leddy My Aunt Eileen And James Leddy (My Grandfather) and all the McDonough Sisters May, Dolly and of course Aunt Helen, Missy and Rory and My Cousins the Wards and the Keoughs.

Simon and Mary Cronin (Grandma) Uncle Tommy, and my Godfather Uncle Jack and My Uncle Bill Scanlon and Aunt Jenny and and Aunt

Winnie and Aunt Carol and Johnny -Boy and Grace Gambino. And all the Leddy and Cronin's that were a major part of my Brooklyn experience.

The best cousins anyone could ever be blessed with.

The Gardner's Uncle Billy Aunt Joan, Cousins Mary Beth, Billy, Bobby,Lori Ann, Ellen and Dori ..Jo Thomas and the Nee Family as well.

The McMahons Uncle Don and Aunt Marilyn, Donna, Brian, Mary ..Jo, and Erin and

The Aneses Uncle Ted Aunt Joan Charlie, Micky, Teddy,Billy and Tommy

The Nelsons..Who were like cousins to me and my Family ...Glen, Pat, Glen, Michael, and Christopher ...My memories of "The Shack" will live on forever in my mind.

The 55Th Between Ave L&M Street Family....
The Barkers Harold Pat Sissy. Buster, George and Stephanie
The DeVitos, Mike Connie..Michael Peter and Phyllis
The Capozzellas John Edna Skippy, Bo,Janie and Tinky
The Duvals Dennis.Everett Joe, Eddie and Noreen
The Oswalds Ozzie
The Brennans Roger and Margie, Michael Linda, Phillip Johnny and James
The Williams Ed and Mrs Williams(! never knew her name it was always Mrs Williams to me)
The Eppolitos Donna, Debbie, Peter and Anthony
The Petrolongos
The Franzas Johnny and Cynthia
The McLindens Denise
The Nelsons..Who were like cousins to me and my Family ...Glen, Pat, Glen, Michael, and Christopher ...My memories of "The Shack" will live on forever in my mind.
The Connors
The Robinsons Mrs Robinson, Kenny Doug and Sister Mary-Beth
The Kennedys

The Brackens
Nick Dimple
The Longs Kate and Maureen
The Harrington Michael Raymond
The Shorts Pat Kristina
The McKennas Judy Tamarin
The Baxter's Gerry and Alice, Gerry Kevin Timothy and Mary Alice
The Mohans
The Kiernans Gerry, Christine Dumarest Larry and Otis
The DeVitos Danny and Judy
The Fucqas Joe Justine, Donny and Joey
The Miellos ..Mrs Miello Dom, Fran Denise and Michael
The Muellers
The Savinos Stephanie Nick and Jimmy
The Geracis
The Redas John Marie and Diana Patricia, Maryann Debra, Gregory and Joann
Mrs Timmons
Mrs Murphy
The Donovan Sisters
The Flaherty's Pattie McNamara Donovan
Anna Bananna
The Scotts Kenny, Judy,Linda and Everett (Boobie)
The Rasmussen
The Browns Marybeth Colleen Chris
The McHenrys Marty Ann Michael Fran Gerard Brian
The Spinellis Patty Kenny Joey Staci and Joanne
The Joyces Maura Eileen PJ Michael
The Poidervans
The Harsons Louise Theresa Robbie
The Kiernans Christine Larry Otis
The Corlonis Armondo Grace Eddie Michael Johnny
Mrs Ritter
The Tolans Agnes Joe Judy Keith Barbara Terry
The Smiths Danny Ann Chris Michael Danny
The Deces Dorothy
Mrs Perrotta
Millie Cynthia Garcia

The McNamara Betsey Pattie
The Bolgnese Family
The Soriano Family
The Rutherford Family
The Adrian Family
The Vitti Family
The Coffey Family

The Sundbyes Alice Cathy Buckaroo Johnny Patty Joe Michael
The Squicciarinis Millie Michael Bella Thomas and Marguerite
55TH Between M&N
Billy Kevin Joanne Timmy Patty Butler
Carol Kasten
Jimmy Matty Jack Maryellen Denise Michael Burke
Robin Shea
Jimmy Quranta
Mike Danchuck
Michael BettyAnn Lorraine Lavin
Lorretta Stephan LaBryerre
Geralyn Joyce Janet Fotie
Jimmy Patrick O'Reilly
Buddy Kathleen Dorothy Thomas Williams
Andy Cardello
Sean Coleen Kerry Kevin Cannon
Doug Greg Hamilton
Michael Caroline Accardi
Eddie Diane Schultz
Janet Kerrigan
Tommy Jimmy Boston
Bob Buchowski

Tommy Votto
The Lavins Michael Betty Ann and Lorraine

My Long Island Family
Frank and Terry Riess "Mrs R"

Lucille Jeanie Patty Bruce and the Gestl Family
Frank, Patty, Nicole, Jeremy, Joanna, and Daniel Riess
John Sharon, John Michael Nikki and Parker Flynn
Willie Barrie Kacie Kyle Kalin Riess
My Best Friend Christopher McCormack
Pat and Tracy Lynch
Ally Flaherty
Annie Gloeggler

The "L" Park Crew"
Billy Whalen Tim Whalen
Danny and Joey Orally
John Kitty Steve Zacharias
Leo Sara Joe Sal Josephine and Martha Porcaro
Didi Engle
Michelle Rosen
John Tomasso
Frankie Pizzola
Tony Elana Fran and Katina Rabias
Larry Rosen
Beany Greenberg
Gary Lasky
Danny Mancha
David West
Ray John (Hobie) Noreen Hart
Rich Gerald and Jeff McCarthy
Steve (Mason) Tommy Herrera
Joi and Jodi Guarino
Michelle Carolyn Bivona
Dorothy Malysz
Ronnie Bruno
Steve Rowan
Joe Fran and Maria Mangano
The Kuzinskis Bruce Maryann Anthony Michael Scott Missy Matty Greg
John
The Atwoods John Jane Raymond Gerald and Elaine
Linda Olivo

Carol Bozza
Joyce Cataldo
Louis (Black) Camille Napolitano
Lawrence Louie (Blonde) Melody Irene Napolitano
Nancy Napolitano
Boo Boo Lynch
Mike Pacella
Percy Percicano
The Kabaks
Elyse Weidermeyer
Dana Forsythe
Susan Debbie Liz Richie Schimdt
Toni-Ann Eddie Joyce Cataldo
Christine Destefano
(Budda) Tom Debbie Norine John Lombardi
Danny Larry Bobby Debbie Joan Taylor
Fran McPhillips
Peter Lafrosia
Joey Richie Kathy Borgia
Jimmy (Soupy) Campbells
Linda Ditta
Madeline Collette
Joe MaryAlice Marty Canning
John Mulroony
Donna Schultz
Francine Muffaletto
Lisa Winner
Irene Tommy Robert Jacqueline Beth Cuccurullo
Freddy Storz
Johnny Tmmy Black
Angelo Danny Billy Stallone
Billy Kern
Mike Nowicki
Joey Testa
Charlie Abe Harvey Ruben Karo
Gina Collica
Greg LoVerde
Kathleen Wilkerson

Loretta Campbell
Butchie Donna Iacobelli
Betty Ann and Buddy Howe
William Kathy Hickey
Peter Bolognese
Tommy Connolly
Karen and Camille Clarelli
Tom Daly
Donna Cavaliere
Kim Salmon Butler
Donna Guida
Mike Susie Pacella
Kathleen Farrell
Louis LaRubio
Michael Bracci
Al Loschiavo
Debbie Danny Welch
Pat Campbell
Mike Kileen
Russell Debbie Cunningham
Sam Nancy Totillo
Theresa Golden
The Scalavinos
Celeste Losqardro
(Suzifuscaldo) Sue Fuscaldo
Anthony Monaco
Karen Edward Leddy
Stassi Christina Steven Papavasiliou
Judy Cavaliere
Mike Galatti
Steve Rowan
Nancy Jimmy Bross
Maria Marzullo
Richie Ciavolino
Michael DeFranco
Nick Ciminelli
Joey LaLima
Terrence Chris Mullins

Bobby Mc Gloclklin
Mike Stabile
Herb Woram
Pudgy Walsh
Richie Biglin
Dave Hespe
Andrew Fezza
George Dukas
Daniel Slammer Cunningham
Billy Tommy Ann Adrien
Robert Stephen Miss Santangelo
Rich Pileggi
Lou Gerlando
Pat Di Giacomo
Thomas Palmer
Mary DiFede
Mike Santanella
Anthont Senter
Patty Joey Testa
Chris Rosenberg
Roy DeMeo
Joe Masseria
Sandi Parrotta
George Serota
Jeff Binder
Hymie Karp
Mike Kahn
Richie Greco
Jack Newman
Arnold Okun
Benny the Presser
Marcel Goldfarb
Doug Kreytak
Artie Larson
Artie Cravitt
Lenny Schindler
Louis Mintz
Donna Calligiuri

Brian Franca
Susan LaMonica
George Ram
Bobby Bastos
Peggy Irene Allyson Flood
John Ferraro
Rick Carracappa
Donna DeSilva
Lynn Olds Heaney
Sean Gannon
Dan Layne
John Castronova
Jane John Raymond Gerald Atwood
Patricia Katie Danny Michael Mullady
Stacy Papa
Doreen Doe
Gerri Wilson
Jamie Perri
Sean McAllister
Buddy Raab
Nancy Cavaliere
Doreen TC Rivezzo
Joanne Guastaferri
Eddie Bernardo
Sonny Audrey Maria Peter Salvato
Deena Trusso
Eddie Fahey
Rosie Cassano
Ralph Toni James Peter Marina Bussola
Tom Cappiello
Kevin Dorney
Phil Hannigan
John Connerly
Mike Wilson
Michael Berkowitz
Michael Marianne DeVirgillis
John Layne
Mike Honey Petrucelli

Donald Hannigan
Sal Cutrona
Stephen Hunter
Sparky Sparling
Michelle Karkas
Christine Ward
Karen Ferrone
Maurenn Skully
Beverly Lynch
Frank Holt
Emily Jay Litteri
Lenny Debbie Cary Sclafani
Jackie Marty and Fr. McGowan
Kevin Dillion
John O'Brien
Jimmy Galatro
Chris Vaccarello
Kathie Steele
Nicky Charles Parascondola
Billy Ray Kevin Ednie
Susan Ansalone
Linda Deserio
Matty Sullivan
Anthony Maryann Labita
The Guest Family
The Ednie Family
The Keenan Family
The Michaels Family Margaret
The Dillion Family
The Weirbrock Family
The Jacobson Family Carole and Kevin

MQH Class of '74

Katie Mullady	Nick Blend
Timmy Butler	Patrice Kawas
Richard Lama	Tony Fiore
Christine DeStefano	Carolyn Chieco
Lori Cook	Debbie Noble
Carole Jacobsen	Donna Cox
Catherine Higgins	Lori Merritt
Joe Duvale	Joann Petrucci
Diana Pimenta	Lisa Jo Catapano
Diane Harrington	Kevin McLoughlin
Gerri Shea	Robert Weingrad
Connie Basciano	Kevin Leddy
Cathy Lampasi	Robin Shea
Jane Piccerill	Tim McCluskey
Don Neubauer	Joe Canning
Diane Rufo	Robert Fitzpatrick
Josephine Vigliarolo	Ron Galassa
Maryellen Burke	Glenn Scialdoni
Hugh Doherty	Maryellen Regan
Ed Norris	Susan Lewis
Patty Reda	Anthony Lorenzo
Taryn Tominello	Kathy Murray
Pat Branley	Jacqueline Ward
Carmine Carrierio	John Heck
Mary Catherine	Kenny Parcell
Brennan	
Mike Ginnettino	Ronald Lewis
Linda Jones	Jimmy Lorenzo
Anthony Patrizio	Maureen Parcells
Dorothy Williams	Stephanie Pavatta
Lorraine Lavin	James Bussola
Tom Hart	Barbara Richter
Anthony Monaco	Barbara Facovic
Rod Imbriani	Jimmy Greene
Carol Bozza	Ray Acetta

Jimmy Cook

James Bussola

Camille Clarelli

Christine Resta

Janet Wagner

Debbie Cox

Mike Giannettino

Tom Hart

Jimmy Ginther

John Olsen

Michael DeVirgihis

Thomas Famularo

Ralph Granada

Bobby Canzoneri

Karan Nemser

Gigi Tonachio

Alan Linderman

Alan Marshall

Howard Mintzer

Orsula Voltis Karpathios

Brooklyn Donna

Gloria Zangrillo

Rick Caruba

Sal Ambrosino

Lynn Scarfuto

Roslyn Heisler

Ernie Zimmerman

Al Tannenbaum

Eileen York

Ann McDermott

Brooklyn Butch

Therese C. Knight

Liz Patrone Freeman

Pat Tierney

MaryLou LaMarco

Jimmy Quranta

Ann Adrian

Joe Clark

Kathy Needham

Lisa Russo

Mary LaRusso

John O'Brien

Peter Olsen

Joseph Portagallo

Peggy Faulkner

Theresa Dunn

Michael Abbondanza

Patricia Bertucelli

Laura Winter

Linda Panasci

Patricia Campanelli

Alice McGoldrick

John Wronka

Janet Pope

Diane DiOrio

Mary Veech

Kathy Crowley

Valerie Hintze

Rick Jaworsky

David Podesta

Ellen Birmingham Massaro

Joyce Canner Burrafato

Patricia Sherman

Diane Aherne

Katie Horkan

Kathy Mancusi Bishop

Laura Brusca

Brother Robert Falcone

Fr. Fullem

Dawn Straccia

Francine Cundari

Vic Grillo Sr.

Frances Incorvaia Garofalo

Angela Incorvaia Moore

Joe Magnani

RoseAnn Benizzi Drew

Carol Santoro

Carol Gearns LoPorto

Josephine Nardello

Andrew Moriello

Antonio Lorenzo

Rose Cassarino Sandelman

Denise Citarella

Joey Mason

Andrew Barone

Odilia Iaquinto

Alan Brody

Thomas Bragg

Alan Diaz

Tim Black

Johnny Black

Geraldine Flaherty

Jeanne Peterson Wallace

Phil Rizzuto

Gary Kasan

Jody Benson

Esther Kleiman Rofe

June Cravett

Edward Hershey

Nancy Duehring

Marilyn Stanton

Denise Starr

Linda Gaffney

Carol Meyers

Nancy Cohen

Joe Ciccone

Hilda Lopez

Mali Weinand

Paulette Young

Herb Steel

Amie Donofrio

Virginia McPeak

Kathy Kassover

Robyn Nicol Fahey

Brooklyn Tony Rodriguez

Sandy Sinclair

Judy Eigen Sarch

Julie Scalamandre

Maureen Maguire

Ronald Semaria

Georgia Coppola

Lorraine Kruk

Stewart Knee

Jeanne Stieglitz

Lillian Lombardi

Lois Dessot

Kathy Dykstra

Richie Ciavolino

Eli Goldstein

Lisa Cali McGrade

Linda Ardigo

Marilyn Fogliano

Joe Rosato

Kevin Ronayne

Maria Josephine
Barbara Leibovitch
Luger

Marie Savage

Michael Latora

Toni Soldano
Riccardo

Ila Mendelson
Fishman

Dorothy LaRose

Jennifer Garofalo

Linda Greco Eckstein

Jack Caliendo

Mary Ann Neglia

Denise Sardo
Brunetti

Catherine Aiello
Rocco

Anne Merlino Tredici

Merry Zullo Gaeta

Josephine Tecia
Cincotta

Simone DiPaola

Edith Serafin

Madeline DeMartino
DeAmicis

Louise Wisniewski
Chicchetti

Jeannine Ali

Antoinette Guerra
Rubin

Phillip Cannizzaro

Roseann DiMaria

William Rohr

Anna Marie Vitanza

Linda Cannici
Valentin

Nello Caltabiano

Lucy Rentas

Elissa Ieye

Laurie Lig

Linda Rosario

Melissa DeJoseph

Diane Fuzzi Izzo

Patricia McGuiness

John Antis

Ellen Musto

Maggie Deming

Pricilla Pendola

Sandra Nasar Maxwell

Marian Vitale

Kelly Starr

Lulu Gentile

Sue Cast

Allyson Malliband Compitello

Patricia Sondergeld

John Soriano

Vinny Soriano

Roger Lundy

Heather Cassidy

Nadine Colontuono Balestrino

Annette Guida

Bridget Looney

John Chiarmonte

Ralph LaMonda

Linda Weiss

Dottie Dondero Lauer

Michael Mellon

Helen McCarthy

Donnie Spano Militello

Celeste Ferraioli Oswald

Paula Sindel Yehezkel

Rise Bache

Sandy Wexler

Lola White

Donna Sellitti Carrera

Randy Brahm

Janet Buono

Bob Goff

Vicki Clark

Carole Soler

Dale Tilley Vani

MaryAnn Trapani

Ilyssa Esgar

Joann Matteo

Dorothy Massimillo Pantano

Mike Norwicki

George Serota

Paul Monteleone

Mary Theresa Howell Doheny

Celeste Basmangy Valle

Jackie Quadrino Russo

Theresa Capelli Casey

Pat Campbell Campisi

Dave DelVecchio

Mark Scalli

Suzanne Ostopowitz Killen

Dianne Caruso Russo

Tracy Crossan

Helen Schwartz
Thomas
Benee Knee-Holiday
Richy Phillips

Susan Pickens
Phil Hannigan
Janet Dort Miceli

Phyllis L. Sabin
Kendall
Donna DeVito
Gladys
Thompson-Manni
Lynne Shapiro

Marie Bellucci
Danny Stallone
Nancy Totillo
Sammy Totillo
Steve Zacharias
John Zacharias

Kitty Zacharias
Michael DiFedi
Conni Chiaramonte
Debra Malone
Danner
Linda Ditta
Judy Tamarin

Lynn Sinisgalli
McDonald
Peter Mulligan
Stephanie Selix
Kellerman
Lois Dessot

Francine Muffaletto
Manzo
Mike Pacella
Gail
Kulman-Szwarcglas
Sharon Rasmussen
Frank Barone
Rita Burnstein
Friedman
Ellen Greene

Amy Applebaum
Marian Vitale

Lori Mangano
Bimonte
Rick Ansolone
Daniel Dowd
Judy Kopp Irving
Myra Chesner
Ellyn McKenna
Sandi Ehrilich
Weingroff
Nan Schwartz Dalton
Fran McCabe
RoseMary Farrell
Natalie Markowitz

Roger Smith
Sheryl Frankel
Hershkowitz
Lynn Gorse

Thomas Montegari
Judy Bradner
Hickman
Arthur Broder

Derek Flament

Lorraine Posner Zapin

Gail Nunsbaum Schwartz

David Partenio Sr.

Susan Schwartz Leigh

Janice Baran Blatt

Diane Udell

Donna Schulz Penney

John Soriano

Karen Clarelli

Mary Alice Canning Spinella

Carol DeLia-Brooks

Dan Gioia

Victoria Gioia

Tom O'Hara

Kathy Hickey Fox

Tommy Tierney

Angela DeSilva

Keith Cannon

Loretta Campbell

Sal Russo

Amiee Bingham

Barbara Dowd

Margaret Catalano

Kathy Purcell Walker

Patricia Gannon Hunt

Dennis McKeon

Maureen Kleinman

Janet Kerrigan

Diane Schultz

Laura Stadler

Phillip White

Betsy McNamara

John Montaniz

Kathy Montaniz

Deana Trusso

Tom Daily

Buddy Howe

BettyAnn Howe

Brenda Marion Acevedo

Lori Chiaramonte Crawford

Stephen Cummins

Susie Pacella Otero

Phil Amato

JulieAnn Savino Colella

Frances Ficano

Dominic Cusimano

Clementine Catapano

Brian Stedman

Christina Papavasillou Caputo

Debbie Welch

Eileen Mooney

Beverly Holzer

Sal Meringolo

Elyse Wiedemeier

Bunny Mathenny

Gina Saggio

Kevin Dorney

Ralph Grilli

Larry McGarrigle

Jerri Belford

Linda DeSerio

MariAnne Berlofsky

Pat Stange

MaryAnn Browning

Michelle Teasdale-Beattie

Susan LaMonica

Joe Cutrona

Theresa Scutari

Tommy Dowd

Eileen Dowd

Grace Heck

Brian Franca

Carole Intravia

William Dowd

Maryellen McKeon

Dana Feeney

Peggy O'Brien Mauro

Grace Lubrano

Victor John Rosati Sr.

Marilyn Brock Finnelli

Gil Mastrovito

Kathy Neubauer

Tracy Neubauer

Donna Schiumo

Erin Cannon

Ann Adrian

Louise Molinari

Barbara Feibel

Susan Anasalone

Edward Dowd

Kevin Jacobson

Laurie Sundbye

Kathy Dowd

Elizabeth Lavin

Richie Tepedino

Vickie Lopardo Canavan

Chris Meyer

Chuck Bisang

Susan Molinari

Michael Molinari

Larry Musso

Bob Gandley

Pat McSorley

Debbie Thorsen Peterson

Laura Ferraro Birro

John Ferraro

Donna Townsend

Renee Tracy Askew

MaryJo Carnacchio

Michael Gruber

Patricia Hughes

Espie Tamayo

Nancy Amoroso

Margaret Lyons

Maureen Ferry

Patricia Scott Amerino

Diane Aherne O'Dougherty

RoseAnn Militano DePalma

Diane DeOrio

Anne Thomson
Kimmy Rutherford

Scott Hinz

Mary Lizardi
Robert Herrera
Thomas Montegari
Maureen Monahan Arafa
Ellen Blackhall
Caryl Estes

Hfr Develin
Joann Fischetti McCormack
Rhonda Dunning
Joyce Serpico-Scalzo
Rick Fontaine
Lorraine Venturino Luban
Susan Duffy DeModna
Barbara Blackhall
Sherry Roth
Mike Petti
Dana Crow Forsythe
John Mulrooney
Doreen Rivezzo
Richie (Bill's Bar)
Gina Collica
Tommy Lenzo
Liz Patrone Freeman
Brian Green
Brian Henricksen
Rob Racalbuto
Richard Schmidt

Mary Askins Phillips
Barbara Buonocore Booker
Roseanne McGuire Meyers
Judy Bartolomeo
Maryann Trapani
Maryann Torrelli
Anthony Dragonetti

Joanne Corbett
Brooklyn Tony Rodriguez
Bill Kern
Deborah O'Shea

Erin Marley
Peggy Flood
Eddie Fahey
Colleen Cannon

Tommy Connolly

Alan Diaz
Billy Stallone
Gina Ferrari
Sean Cannon
Kerry Cannon
Christine Holahan
Vinny Soriano
Theresa Golden
Cathy Staiano
Pat Daly
Janet Fotie
Joyce Fotie
Geralyn Fotie
Nick Mastrangelo

Christopher Freese
Lisa Ferraro
McHenry
Carol Casten
Susan Castagna
Isaiah Bethea

Simone
Frank Trifoli
Stacy Ann Miller
Robert Roberto
Andy Voght
George Zimmer
Jerry Goodstein
Gail Goodstein
Alan Satcowitz
Karen Sactowitz
Victor "Paco" Claxton
Karen Russell
Robert Russell
Naomi Stevenson
Keith Banks
Eleanor Banks
Richard "Knowledge"
Harris
Stephanie Harris
Nadine Kornegay
Michelle Corbett
Keith Gholson
Didi Turner
Steve Herrera
Willie Herrera
Chris Crowley
Connie Crowley
Donna Schulz
Ron Morse

Charles Scolnik
Mohammed
Mohammed
Mohammed Ibrahim
Shanti Persaud
Warren "Coach"
Fuller
G- Man
Anthony Ruff
Fernando Santiago
Sonny Brown
Ellisha Haynes
Daniel O'Brien
Kathy Borgia
Richie Borgia
Joey Borgia
Joe Christodora
Pat Dougherty
Ann Dougherty
Tommy Dougherty
Dave Harrow
Jimmy O'Leary
Jimmy Durfee
Mindy Lyons

Madeline Collette
Doreen Rivezzo
Robin Hatzidakis
Patty Dodge
Ieasha Moneek
Kathleen Farrell
Howard May
Mike Fortini
Duke Fortini
Susan Pickens
Uncle Ken
Willoughby

Manny Reyes

Recovery Room
Ciara Dempsey
Donal
Maria
April
Pete "Double H"
Guinnane
Dave
Alex
Steve
Bobby
Kevin
Mary Burroughs
Patterson
Shemar Byrd
Kareem Byrd
Billy Anese
Tommy Anese
Kelly Hay
Sue Czarecki
Jeff Nuspliger
Carol Stillwagon
Dave Stillwagon
The Allen Family
John Portelli
Pat McDonald
John McDonald
Robert Bjelke
The Scalavino Family
Jimi Savino
James Savino
Carey Savino
Doreen Giannettino
Ron Semaria

Aunt Estelle
Willoughby
Paul Willoughby
Keith Willoughby
Kathleen Wilkinson
John Ferranti
Lisa Ferranti
Gina Ferranti

Anthony Russo
Charles Parahawk
Mt. Lake
Uncle Ted Anese
Aunt Joan Anese
Charlie Anese

Nicky Anese
Teddy Anese
Eileen Dowd
Mary Fealey
Julann Rennish
Linda Carrozza
Cornelia DeCarpio
Greg Denino
Lorraine Sorenson
Eve Romano Rea
Sue Gylnn Volpe
Gerard Quinn
Virginia Cantone
Gina Saggio
Mary Moran
Lilian Lepard
Jimmy Galatro
Kevin Dorney
Fran Imbriale
Maria Mistrulli

Angela Ballah Ucciardino

Marc Cararo

Irene Cararo

Theresa Beshara

Roly Penn

Ruth Kweller Cohen

The Losquadra Family

Jae Fiore

Phil Fahey

Grace Gervasi

The Dowd Family

Sean Massi

Dan Layne

Christine Maher

Janet Kerrigan

Mike Santanella

Pete Smith

Daniel Dowd

Jack O'Dowd

Jeff Jimenez

David Lusardi

Peter Bolognese

Vicki Clark

Barbara Smith Frank

Donna Iacobelli

Butch Iacobelli

Jerry Belford

Mag Parenti

Pat Ahearn

The Ahearn Family

RoseAnn Giannone

The Caracappa Family

Bruno Zauhar

The Cavaliere Family

Don Hannigan

The Fotie Family

Joanne Guastaferri

Peter Lusardi

Christine Fahey

Kim Salmon Butler

The Flood Family

Marilyn Zayfert

Richy Phillips

Louis LaRubio

Mike Nowicki

Donna Guida

Terri Breslau

Brian Steadman

Vito Antuofermo

Nick Antuofermo

Brooklyn Domino

Florence Ann

Floyd Calloway

The Kollin Family

Tommy DeVivio

Marc Lunio

Sherry Roth

Maximillan Roth

Maryann Smith

Joseph Giardina

Pat Strange

Mike LaCava

The LaCava Family

Ralph LaMonda

Gina Provenzano

Helen Proveromo

Steven Ferretti

Ann Beth Schiffman

Diana Cappiello

John Cappiello

Frankie Sorrentino

Michael Sansone

Thomas Scaduto

The Kuczinski Family

MaryJane Pomponio

Anthony DeLuca

The Cunningham
Family

Debbie Cunnigham

Scott Gallo

Nino's Candy Store

Evan Penn

John F. Morrissey

Dorene Grosso

Judy Carnacchio

Donna Rea

Bridget Looney
Nowicki

Eileen Long Sullivan

Joe Doody

Ralph Grilli

Patty Biolsi

Theresa Scutari

Sal Bartolomeo

Jim Powderly

Brian Duval Gambino

Eileen Boone Gaffey

Jay Moccaldi

Brian Franca

Joe Masseria

The Chiaramonte
Family

Anthony Messina

Rita Naplitano
Barrone

Irene Naplitano

Melody Naplitano

Louis Naplitano

Lawrence Naplitano

Eileen Gregan

Kathleen Colgan

Rich DiMino

Judy Brackner
Hickman

Richie Ciavolino

John C. Donnell

Maryellen Pokowitz

The Caiazzo Family

Larry McGarrigle

RoseAnn Bassolino

The Gotti Family

Eileen Sillivan Irish

Perry Russell

Doris Dee

The Karkis Family

Linda Losi

Patty Flaherty

The Flaherty Family

The Sundbye Family

Arlene Prado

Cynthia Brennan
Dougherty

Pat Lynch

Tracy Lynch

Linda Carol Ehrlich

Suzi Fuscaldo

Anthony Pergola
Libra DiCallo
The Herrara Family
Victor Scotto
The Scotto Family
Kathryn Thomas
Cortelyou
Christine Piccio
Petrie
Arlene Rothstein
Francine Lampasi
Marian Vitale
Dale Tily
The Lavin Family

Freddy Claps

JoAnn Hull Fyfe
The Hull Family
Theresa Campbell
LoGatto
Stephanie Seliy
Lorraine Crawley
Larry Rosen
Michelle Rosen
Linda McNulty
Cerenzio
Nancy Napiltano
Paul Mosher
Mike Petruccelli
Debby Gentile
Marguerite Cestro
Honey Petruccelli

Donna Pecci Volpetti
Maria Tammaro

The Fuscaldo Family
John Lompanbo
Tim Whalen
Bill Whalen
Kenny Meyer
Scott Bellocchio

Susan Ansaline

Mark Kennish
Gina M. Pappalardo
Dana Feeney
Julienne Giovanniello
Angela Bongiorno
Caiazzo
Carolynn Caffiero
Curtis
Steve Sepe
Greg Denino
Vincent Prezioso

Ann Prezioso
Kathy Sivon
Jackie Merz Gerace
The Merz Family
JuliAnn Budney

Lisa Vulpis
The Vulpis Family
The Kabak Family
Shira Gelman
Flannigan
Danielle Kennish
O'Donnell
Steve Lombardozzi
The Lombardozzi
Family

Carol Mangine Sepe

William PIncus
Bill Parenta
John Ferraro
The Ferraro Family
Loretta Moraco
Roger Lundy
Tommy Dee
Billy Barclay
Jimmy Barclay
Maureen Barclay
The Barclay Family
Mike Giannetino
The Giannetino
Family
Tom Palmer
Krissy Hughes
Chris Fountaine
The LaBruyele
Family
The Alessi Family
Scott Gollubier
Patricia
Scott-Amerino
Sandi Parrotta
Charmante
The Parrotta Family
Rami Lasker
David J. Partenio Sr.
Joe Turner
Clair McGuckin
Leface
Anthony Carvino
Tara Urbanowicz
Rockin Raymond
Linda Agro
D'Onofrio
Michael Gruber

John Alfieri
Louis Alfieri
Tom Lombardi
Norine Lombardi
Debbie Lombardi
The Lombardi Family
Liza Yonus
Margaret Anne Serpe
Jeanne Caneiro
Gina Acito Herbert
Rob Poidevin
The Poidevin Family
Etty Reisca

Barbara Kivet
Jenn Gluck
Sheila Dillon Higgins
Danny Tracy

The Tracy Family
Sean Gannon
Gary Alaimo

Laura DiGiacomo

Janet Rublin
Eric Rassten
Bill Dougherty
Tony DeMatteo
Joe Pece

The Wilkerson
Family
Kevin Dillion
The Dillion Family
Nancy Barberi
Susan Henrich
Wallabre
Tommy Cronin
Kevin Cronin
The Cronin Family
Todd Marcus
Stacy Papa
Donna Mario
Judy Lee
Krissy Hughes
Marie Graziano
Shery L. Kraut Gersh
Paulette Russo Lepore
Joseph Volpi Sr.
Joann Cestaro
Lopiccolo
Joseph Coffey
Linda Scapa
Eve Romano Rea
Ellen Parsons
Judy Rothen Berg
Arthur Broder
Janice Baran Blatt
Sue Lawrence
Rita Bernstein
Friedman
Carol Treuel Faraci
Carol Louise
Cathy Duncan
Eileen Gillen
Elyse Wiedemeir
Ellyn McKenna

Lorraine Posner
Zapin
Stephanie Savino
Ferraro
The Savino Family
Francine Muffaletto
Manzo
Lisa Ann Fasano
Michael Kelly
George Patsis
Dawn McPhillips
Diana Hermann
John Manning
Sal Curto
Brian Green
Dominic Cusimano
Eileen DeMarco
DiLorenzo
Jo Beth Persicano
The Persicano Family
Stu Vogel
Paul Miccolupi
Joan Butler
Mickey Mike Wallace
Karla George
Carolyn Vignola
Taylor
Alan Marshall
Barbara Leibovitch
Lugery
Timothy Judge
Dale Tilley Vani
Robbie Robinson
Victoria Gioia
Aldo Bapaci
Dot Hall Hanlon
Joan Fleur

Silver Fox
Claudett Thomas
Brantley
Will Gardiner
Regina Chambers
Jerome Merkerson
Rosanne Forsyth
Lisa Harary Rosen
Frankie Sollerito
Joe Testa
Bill Bonanno
The Bonnano Family
Rich Lama
Tony Lama
Fred Lama
The Squicciarini
Family
Liz Silverman Corrar
Barbara Luonco
Krinsky
Mary Difede
Michael Difede
The Difede Family
Richard Resnick
Maura Joyce Eagle
The Joyce Family
Marion Connolly
The Connolly Family
Lou Vitalo
Joey Comes
Donna Garcia Fama
The Neubauer Family
Susan Hersh
Kurt Issac
Debra Bell
Nancy Calvarino
Anthony Pompanio

Dennis McKeon
The McKeon Family
Steven Santangelo
Robert Santangelo
The Santangelo
Family
Danny Fazzingo
James Longo
Paul Punzone
Bill Croce
Maria Croce
Nan Schwartz Dalton
Christine Savino
Fiorenza
Erin Cannon Steiler
Kerry Cannon
The Cannon Family
Camille C
Lisa Scala
Maria Labita
Anthony Labita
The Labita Family
Michael Merrett
Lori Merrett
Jim Bomatakis
Karen Rispoli
Kathy Williams
Dottie Williams
Buddy Williams
Thomas Williams
The Williams Family
Rod Imbriannia
Dennis Fulbrook
Sherry Paige
Goldberg
John S. Hershkowitz
Jimmy Bross

Nancy Bross
The Bross Family
Jerry Walsh
Tommy Guiffre
Vic DiBitetto
Jim KIernan
The Kiernan Family
Tinamarie Halzer
Dan Quigly
Kellyanne Fahey
Brad Mester
Michael Mellon
Linda Mellon
Joe Spienza
John Borzo
Tony Peluso
Shelle Berk
William Devenport
Tara Hamilton
Mary Lizardy
Diane Rav Kelly
Kimmy Rutherford
Scott Kaplan
Louie Gampero
Michael Sanseverino
Rise Bache
Anna Maria Romano
Gail Kulman
Szwarcelas
Adria Falcon
Lynn Costantino
Cutolo
Irene Dulinda
Gloria Saperstein
Doreen Brusca
Armina
Michelle Di Lisa

Billy De Luca
Barbara Wolpert
Nanci La Gargenne
Gina Farley Preziosa
Donald Townsend
Terry Braci Townsend
The Townsend
Family
The Braci Family
Janet West Grasso
Rita Jeannetti
Moniardo
Celeste Ferraioli
Oswald
Regina Walsh Langan
Terri Ann Kraft
Fran Campbell
Jane Collier
Richie Pileggi
Edward Norris
The Cutrone Family
The Cutrona Family
Aly Moriarty
Steve Zangre Sr.
Cathy Staiano
Caneiro
Norma Vally
Tommy Vatto
Paul Gelsman
Tea Toac
Robbie Schwartz
Paula Sindel
Yehezkiel
Randy Harrison
Virginia McPeak
Frank Ruf
Debra Bell

Alan Diaz
Leann McGovern
Matt McCool
Linda Panasci Eden
Gary Kasan
Dawn Straccia
Ross Faillico
Rose Cassano
Sheily Monchik
Linda Gioia
Bob Goff
Rich Romano
Joe Bezzina
Mike Iannuzzi
Peter Lee
Bill Kern
George Jones
Joan Farruggio
Chiochetti
Marlene West
Joyce Jones
Kathleen McGronty
Dawn Cohen
Beverly Axel Smith
Alyse Greenberg
Giancola
Patricia M. Gannon
Hunt
Butch Sikes
Donna Petrucci
Nicolette Borgia
Shiela Sweeney
Camille DeStefano
Jeff Jimenez
John Bisang
Maryanne Giordano
Andrea Glindmeir

Hilda Lopez
Barbara J. McCauley
Robert Fortunado
Matthew LaMarcia
Denise DeNitto Shaw
Michela Morrison
Frank Bassetti
Joey Mason
Michael Brodsky
Jane Piccerelli
Julie Blue Bogorad
Beverly Beck
Sigrun DeRienzo
Thomas Bragg
Jimmy Ginther
The Ginther Family
Dawn Carvino
Linda Olivo
Laura Olds Falcone
Dan Hollihan
Joe Canning
Marty Canning
Maryalice Canning
Camille Clarelli
Karen Clarelli
Carol Indelicato
Nappa
Edward Tuohy
Odilia Iaquainto
Marie Bellucci
Donna Solomita Storz
Theresa Dunn Belk
Diane DeOrio
Walter Mapes
Denise Starr
Linda Gaffney
McDonagh

Judy Sheenberg
MIchael J. Boles
Carol Ann Kase
Janet Dort Micelli
Matt Tedesco

The Butler Family Billy Timmy Kevin Patty
The Williams Kathy, Buddy, Dottie and Tommy
The Labruyere Family Loretta Stephen and Regina
The Cannon family, Keith Sean, Coleen Kerry
The Mangano Family Joe Fran and Maria
The Lavin Family Betty Ann Michael and Lorraine
The Cardello Family
The Danchuk family
The Kastern Family Carol
The Quaranta Family Jimmy
The Fotie Family, Gerylyn Joyce and Janet
The McDonald Family
The Silk Family
The Kerrigan Family
The Schultz Family
The Dockery Family Pat Ann Andrea, Richard Raymond and Tommy
The O'Learys Sheila and Jimmy
John Sutter

CPSIA information can be obtained
at www.ICGtesting.com
Printed in the USA
LVHW030938050721
691875LV00002B/287

9 781543 428599